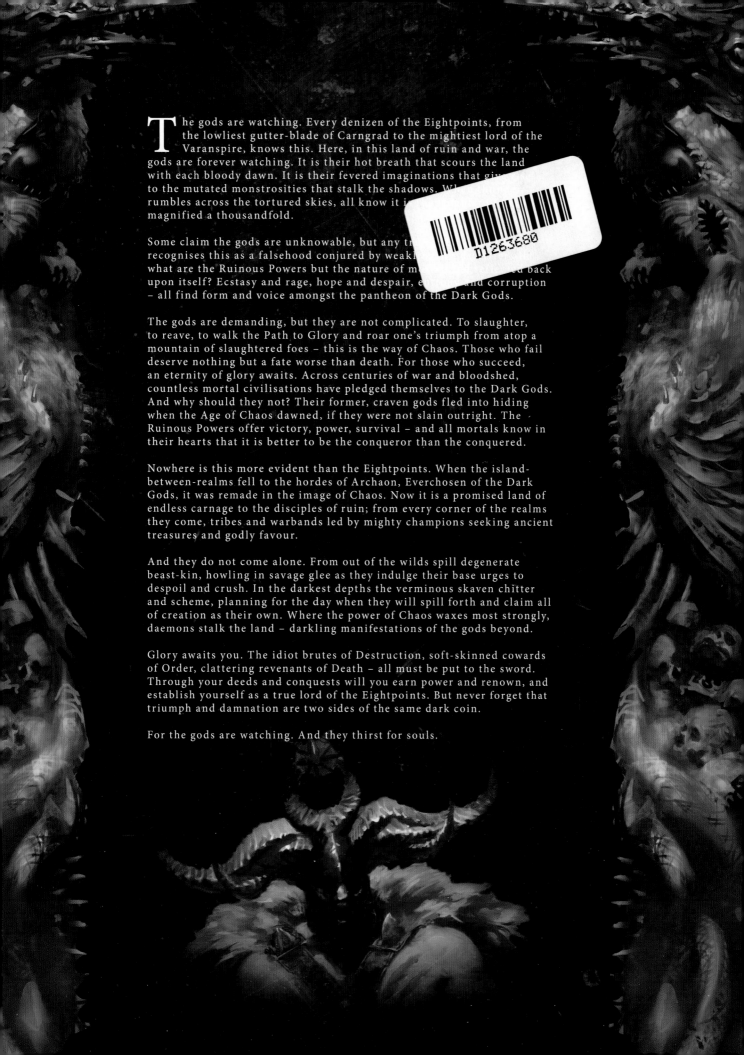

The gods are watching. Every denizen of the Eightpoints, from the lowliest gutter-blade of Carngrad to the mightiest lord of the Varanspire, knows this. Here, in this land of ruin and war, the gods are forever watching. It is their hot breath that scours the land with each bloody dawn. It is their fevered imaginations that give [rise] to the mutated monstrosities that stalk the shadows. Wh[en thunder] rumbles across the tortured skies, all know it i[s their rage] magnified a thousandfold.

Some claim the gods are unknowable, but any tr[ue disciple] recognises this as a falsehood conjured by weak[lings. For] what are the Ruinous Powers but the nature of m[ortality turn]ed back upon itself? Ecstasy and rage, hope and despair, e[ndeavour] and corruption – all find form and voice amongst the pantheon of the Dark Gods.

The gods are demanding, but they are not complicated. To slaughter, to reave, to walk the Path to Glory and roar one's triumph from atop a mountain of slaughtered foes – this is the way of Chaos. Those who fail deserve nothing but a fate worse than death. For those who succeed, an eternity of glory awaits. Across centuries of war and bloodshed, countless mortal civilisations have pledged themselves to the Dark Gods. And why should they not? Their former, craven gods fled into hiding when the Age of Chaos dawned, if they were not slain outright. The Ruinous Powers offer victory, power, survival – and all mortals know in their hearts that it is better to be the conqueror than the conquered.

Nowhere is this more evident than the Eightpoints. When the island-between-realms fell to the hordes of Archaon, Everchosen of the Dark Gods, it was remade in the image of Chaos. Now it is a promised land of endless carnage to the disciples of ruin; from every corner of the realms they come, tribes and warbands led by mighty champions seeking ancient treasures and godly favour.

And they do not come alone. From out of the wilds spill degenerate beast-kin, howling in savage glee as they indulge their base urges to despoil and crush. In the darkest depths the verminous skaven chitter and scheme, planning for the day when they will spill forth and claim all of creation as their own. Where the power of Chaos waxes most strongly, daemons stalk the land – darkling manifestations of the gods beyond.

Glory awaits you. The idiot brutes of Destruction, soft-skinned cowards of Order, clattering revenants of Death – all must be put to the sword. Through your deeds and conquests will you earn power and renown, and establish yourself as a true lord of the Eightpoints. But never forget that triumph and damnation are two sides of the same dark coin.

For the gods are watching. And they thirst for souls.

RUIN AND BLOOD

The Eightpoints is the greatest stronghold of Chaos to be found on the material plane. Ruled by all manner of black-hearted champions and deadly warlords, the lands themselves writhe under the power of ruinous magic. To survive here requires cunning and battle-skill in equal measure, but the servants of the Dark Gods have plenty of both to spare. From heavily armoured tribesmen and scheming cultists to the malevolent skaven and daemonic children of the gods themselves, the warriors of the Ruinous Powers are myriad in aspect, yet all incredibly deadly.

The gods of Chaos demand slaughter and carnage to be wrought in their name. Now, with *Warcry: Agents of Chaos*, you can answer their call. The Bloodwind Spoil is a hotbed of savage rivalries, where power can change hands and champions can rise or fall through the actions of a few fierce warriors. These brutal skirmishes are fast-paced and deadly – with this book, you can forge a warband dedicated to the Dark Gods and plunge right into the thick of the action.

Unsurprisingly, the armies of Chaos possess a breathtaking, anarchic diversity. From animalistic beastmen to armour-clad Chaos Warriors, unnatural daemons to devious skaven, all kinds of malcontents and madmen can be found in the service of the Ruinous Powers. The disciples of Chaos often prefer to deal with things up close and personal, but there's no shortage of playstyles to be found amongst their ranks.

The Disciples of Tzeentch, for example, favour insidious cunning and spellcraft over raw strength, while the merciless Corvus Cabal are shadowy assassins who use agility and surprise attacks to carry the day. Whatever tactics you favour when playing Warcry, you'll find a Chaos warband able to fulfil your desires – and, should you be drawn down dark and sinister paths towards new allegiances, you'll find there are plenty of other factions who may draw your conquering gaze!

Agents of Chaos contains the rules for every fighter and monster dedicated to the Dark Gods that is playable in Warcry. Alongside ability tables that allow you to harness the unique skills and tactics favoured by your warband, this book features complete rules for allying in heroes and thralling monsters to your service – allowing you to expand your warrior bands with more variety than ever before.

Led by great champions and accompanied by ravening thrall-beasts, the warbands of Chaos dominate the Eightpoints. Theirs is an endless battle to earn the favour of monstrous gods – so long as blood and despair, excess and treachery hold sway in these lands, so too will they.

Every would-be champion of Chaos is an individual treading the Path to Glory in their own way; detailed naming and background tables allow you to fully customise the story of your warband and its members. After a few games you'll find that these warriors have almost taken on a life of their own – whether you end up praising their glorious deeds, or cursing their ignoble failures!

For those Warcry gamers who enjoy crafting epic stories and tales through every skirmish, *Agents of Chaos* also features plenty of expansion content for narrative play. New fated quests will see your warband embark on fresh, twisted adventures – from the blood-stained streets of Carngrad to the ruins of fallen empires, you will chase the favour of the gods and battle all manner of challenging foes. Each fated quest allows you to choose the outcome of your campaign, allowing you to intricately develop the story and motivations of your warband while earning powerful rewards. For those seeking greater glories still, new challenge battles allow you to undertake bespoke scenarios designed to truly test your tactical acumen. Should you complete them all, the favour of the Dark Gods will surely be yours!

Now is the age of swords and blood. The Everchosen has sent out the call – new warriors must join his conquering legions, and the enemies of the Dark Gods must be obliterated. Only the strongest, most cunning and most favoured of warbands will prosper in this crucible of war. But should you succeed in drawing the favour of the Ruinous Powers, you will become a legend in your own right. So go – muster your warband, and make war in the name of the gods!

YOUR JOURNEY CONTINUES...

The jaw-dropping expanse of the Eight Realms is all but limitless, and so are the opportunities for exciting games of Warhammer Age of Sigmar.

The Warhammer Age of Sigmar Core Book is your in-depth guide to this fantastical setting. As well as a full and detailed history of the Mortal Realms, from the legendary tales of the Age of Myth to the triumphant crusades of the Stormcast Eternals, you will find a detailed overview of several of the most heavily contested realms. Included within are introductions to each of the Grand Alliances battling across these magical lands, from the tireless legions of Death to the rampaging, howling hordes of Destruction.

Exciting narrative sections, breathtaking world-building and detailed timelines – along with a showcase section presenting beautifully painted Citadel Miniatures in all their glory – will offer plenty of inspiration for your own hobby collection.

Of course, within the pages of the Core Book you will also find the full core rules for the Warhammer Age of Sigmar tabletop game, laying out each stage of a battle in intuitive and easy-to-follow stages. Whether you wish to take on your friends in a balanced competitive match, or prefer to simulate a mythic encounter between fantastical armies in the form of a narrative campaign, this weighty tome provides everything you need to lead your mighty army into battle!

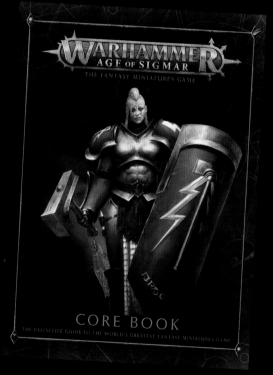

HOW TO USE THIS BOOK

Warcry: Agents of Chaos contains all of the rules you need to field the Warcry warbands of Chaos on the battlefields of the Bloodwind Spoil and beyond.

CHAOS WARBANDS

The rules in this book will often refer to **Chaos warbands**. Every warband in Warcry belongs to one of the following 4 Grand Alliances: **Chaos**, **Death**, **Destruction** or **Order**. A Chaos warband is any warband that has one of the faction runemarks listed in the box below.

In addition, if any rules have the **Chaos** runemark (✹), those rules apply to all Chaos warbands. For example, the Chaos fated quests in this book all have the **Chaos** runemark (✹) and can only be embarked upon by Chaos warbands.

The rules in this book are split into the following sections:

HEROES AND ALLIES

This section explains how to include heroes and allies in your warband.

MONSTERS AND THRALLS

This section contains rules for using monsters in your Warcry battles, including abilities for fighters to use against monsters and abilities for the monsters to use themselves. There are also fighter cards and abilities for the monsters and thralls available to a Chaos warband.

WARBANDS

This section includes all the abilities and fighter cards for Chaos warbands. There are 19 factions available to choose from.

CAMPAIGNS

This section includes 4 Chaos fated quests that any Chaos warband can embark upon.

CHALLENGE BATTLES

This section contains rules for playing challenge battles and includes 6 challenge battles that any Chaos warband can embark upon.

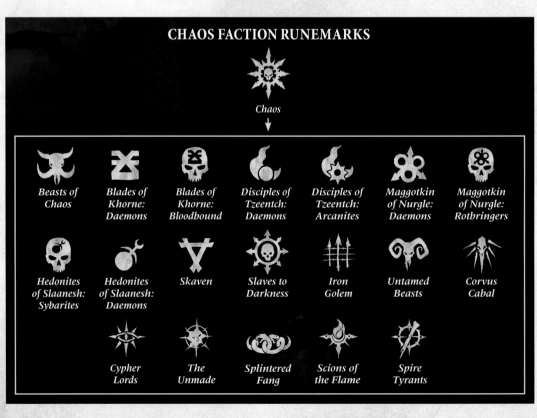

CHAOS FACTION RUNEMARKS

Chaos

Beasts of Chaos	Blades of Khorne: Daemons	Blades of Khorne: Bloodbound	Disciples of Tzeentch: Daemons	Disciples of Tzeentch: Arcanites	Maggotkin of Nurgle: Daemons	Maggotkin of Nurgle: Rotbringers

Hedonites of Slaanesh: Sybarites	Hedonites of Slaanesh: Daemons	Skaven	Slaves to Darkness	Iron Golem	Untamed Beasts	Corvus Cabal

Cypher Lords	The Unmade	Splintered Fang	Scions of the Flame	Spire Tyrants

HEROES AND ALLIES

In the Bloodwind Spoil, each day is a battle for survival. Many warbands seek to make alliances with powerful heroes and champions, for together they stand far greater chance of mastering the wilds than either does alone.

This section provides rules for special types of fighter known as **heroes** and **allies**. These rules allow you to include more than 1 fighter with the **Leader** runemark () in your warband, as well as fighters with a different faction runemark to your warband. This gives you even more ways to theme your warband and make it unique. For example, your band of Iron Golems might have enlisted the aid of a Chaos Sorcerer Lord, or perhaps your Skaven are led by a Plague Priest and his Bringer of the Word disciples.

If you have the *Warcry: Monsters and Mercenaries* expansion, the rules in this section supersede the allies rules in that book.

INCLUDING HEROES AND ALLIES IN YOUR WARBAND

Any fighter with the same faction runemark as your warband and the **Leader** runemark () can be included in your warband as a **hero**.

Any fighter with a different faction runemark to your warband and either the **Leader** runemark () or the **Ally** runemark (○) can be included in your warband as an **ally**. However, warbands can only include allies from the same Grand Alliance. For example, Chaos warbands can only include allies with a Chaos faction runemark.

In addition, fighters with the **Chaotic Beasts** faction runemark (✸) and the **Ally** runemark (○) can be included as allies in Chaos warbands.

There are limits on how many heroes and allies you can include in your warband, depending on the style of game you are playing.

OPEN AND MATCHED PLAY
In open play and matched play, when mustering for a battle, you can include 1 hero or ally in your warband. Heroes and allies cost points just like any other fighter, but allies are ignored for the purposes of the rule that requires all fighters in a warband to share the same faction runemark. In addition, when mustering your warband, heroes and allies are not considered to have the **Leader** runemark ().

NARRATIVE PLAY
In narrative play, heroes and allies can be added to your warband roster like any other fighter, either when you are first filling out your warband roster or during the Add and Remove Fighters step of the aftermath sequence.

Your warband roster can include up to 3 heroes or allies in any combination. When adding fighters to your warband roster, heroes and allies are not considered to have the **Leader** runemark () and do not count towards the maximum number of fighters you can add.

When mustering for a campaign battle, you can include 1 hero or ally from your warband roster for every 2 areas of territory your warband has dominated. For example, if you have 5 areas of dominated territory, you can include up to 2 heroes or allies from your warband roster in your warband for that campaign battle. Heroes and allies cost points just like any other fighter, but allies are ignored for the purposes of the rule that requires all fighters in a warband to share the same faction runemark. In addition, when mustering your warband, heroes and allies are not considered to have the **Leader** runemark ().

If your warband can include thralls when mustering for a campaign battle, any heroes or allies you include in your warband do not decrease the number of thralls you can include, and vice versa.

Like other fighters, heroes and allies can receive destiny levels, players must make injury rolls for them and they can bear lesser artefacts. Heroes can bear artefacts of power and be chosen to become favoured warriors, but allies cannot.

HEROES AND ALLIES NEVER LEAD
When a fighter is included in a warband as a hero or ally, if they have the **Leader** runemark () on their fighter card, this runemark is only used to determine which abilities the fighter can use; the hero or ally is not considered to have the **Leader** runemark () for any other purpose or rule. This means that any rule that refers to the leader of a warband does not refer to any heroes or allies in that warband.

CHAOS ALLIES

In the wilds of the Bloodwind Spoil can be found a myriad of fearsome creatures. These beasts can be bargained with, but a champion must beware, for their souls are as black as any mortal's, and they should never be underestimated.

FOMOROID CRUSHER

Fomoroid Crushers are brutish beasts whose primary purpose is to destroy. Such was not always their fate; long ago they were a race of artisans in thrall to one of the great civilisations of the Allpoints. Worked to the bone by their cruel overseers, they eventually rose up in rebellion. It was a conflict that, through much bloodshed, they eventually triumphed in – only to be enslaved once more by the legions of the Everchosen. The fomoroids were branded with runes of domination, and Archaon relished turning them into forces of unthinking destruction. Fomoroid Crushers are found throughout the fighting pits of Carngrad, and one is occasionally granted to a promising warband by the masters of that dread city. Their affinity with stone and masonry remains, but now they use such tools only to crush and kill, splattering their foes into gory ruin.

FOMOROID CRUSHER ABILITIES	
	[Double] Hurl Masonry: A fighter can use this ability only if they are within 1" of an obstacle. Pick an enemy fighter within 8" of this fighter and roll a dice. On a 3-4, allocate 1 damage point to that fighter. On a 5-6, allocate a number of damage points to that fighter equal to the value of this ability.
	[Triple] Rampaging Charge: Until the end of this fighter's activation, the next time this fighter finishes a move action within 1" of an enemy fighter, pick 1 visible enemy fighter within 1" of this fighter. Allocate a number of damage points to that fighter equal to the value of this ability.
	[Quad] Bloody Trophy: A fighter can use this ability only if an enemy fighter has been taken down by an attack action made by them this activation. The player controlling this fighter immediately gains 1 wild dice that can be used in the hero phase of the next battle round.

OGROID MYRMIDON

The Ogroid Myrmidons are obsessed with war. They are utterly devoted to the art of combat – an echo of their distant past as warriors of the twin-headed God of Destruction, and a reflection of their new status in thrall to the dark powers. Ogroids rule many of the greatest fighting pits of the Bloodwind Spoil, or otherwise travel the tainted lands alone, seeking out the worthiest warriors and most terrifying creatures to slay. Should a warband impress them through skill-at-arms, a Myrmidon may deign to join them for a time. This is a powerful boon indeed, for ogroids are berserk and deadly fighters, exhorting their fellows to greater bloodshed even as they crush their own foes with aplomb.

OGROID MYRMIDON ABILITIES	
	[Double] Berserk: A fighter can only use this ability if 20 or more damage points have been allocated to them. Add half the value of this ability (rounding up) to the Attacks characteristic of the next attack action made by this fighter this activation that has a Range characteristic of 3 or less.
	[Triple] Arcane Fury: Until the end of this fighter's activation, add the value of this ability to the damage points allocated by each critical hit from attack actions made by this fighter that have a Range characteristic of 3 or less.
	[Quad] Blood Marshal: Pick a friendly fighter within 4" of this fighter. Allocate 1 damage point to that fighter. If that fighter is not taken down, they can make a bonus attack action that has a Range characteristic of 3 or less.

MINDSTEALER SPHIRANX

The Eightpoints are stalked by all manner of unsettling beasts, but few are as sinister as the Mindstealer Sphiranxes. Once denizens of Hysh who served the Archmage Teclis, avarice and bitterness proved their undoing, and they struck a terrible bargain that saw them banished from the Ten Paradises and forced to slink into the darkest corners of Archaon's domain. Though a Mindstealer's claws are sharp and its leonine body swift, their true power comes from the third eye upon their forehead. With this mystic orb a Sphiranx can stare into the minds of its foes, plundering knowledge – over which they obsess – or crushing their will to fight, leaving them easy prey for the spiteful beasts.

MINDSTEALER SPHIRANX ABILITIES

	[Double] Telepathic Threatening: Pick an enemy fighter within a number of inches of this fighter equal to the value of this ability and roll a dice. On a 3+, until the end of the battle round, that fighter cannot make move actions or disengage actions.
	[Triple] Dominate Mind: Pick a visible enemy fighter within 6" of this fighter and roll a number of dice equal to the value of this ability. For each roll of a 3-4, allocate 1 damage point to that fighter. For each roll of a 5-6, allocate 3 damage points to that fighter.
	[Quad] Charm: Pick an enemy fighter within a number of inches of this fighter equal to the value of this ability. That fighter cannot activate this battle round.

A band of Khainite Shadowstalkers seek to surround a Mindstealer Sphiranx, little realising that the beast has already plundered knowledge of their weaknesses from their own minds.

MONSTERS AND THRALLS

The Eightpoints is home to more than just corrupted tribesmen. Monsters and beasts of all kinds dwell in this tainted land; the strongest warbands seek to bind such creatures to their will, though that is easier said than done…

MONSTERS

This section refers a type of fighter known as a **monster**. Monsters are fighters with the **Gargantuan** runemark (⬢).

If you have the *Warcry: Monsters and Mercenaries* expansion, the rules in this section supersede the monster rules in that book.

Monsters are subject to the following rules:

DEPLOYING MONSTERS

When monsters are deployed, they must be placed wholly within 5" horizontally of a deployment point instead of wholly within 3".

ACTIVATING MONSTERS

A monster can be activated 3 times in a battle round instead of only once, but each time it is activated, it can make only 1 action instead of 2. Each time a monster is activated, it can use 1 ability before or after its action.

If a monster makes a wait action, its activation immediately ends; the monster is not said to be waiting and the rules for waiting do not apply.

MOVE ACTIONS WITH MONSTERS

A monster can climb and jump like any other fighter; however, if at the end of a move action its base is not wholly on a platform or the battlefield floor, it is said to have fallen.

If a monster is said to have fallen, any part of the model's base can be placed on the point picked by your opponent instead of just the centre.

MONSTER-HUNTING ABILITIES

If any monsters are in play, all fighters except the monsters themselves and fighters with the **Beast** runemark (⬢) can use the **Monster-hunting Abilities** shown opposite.

MONSTERS AND UNIVERSAL ABILITIES

Monsters cannot use universal abilities. Instead, if any monsters are in play, they can use the **Monster Abilities** shown opposite.

MONSTERS AND TREASURE

Monsters can never carry treasure.

THRALLS

On page 15 you will find fighter cards and abilities for 5 types of Thrall. Each of these fighters has the **Chaotic Beasts** faction runemark (⬢) and the **Thrall** runemark (⬢). These fighters can be included in Chaos warbands using the rules on page 49 of the Core Book.

MONSTER-HUNTING ABILITIES

	[Double] Binding Ropes: Pick an enemy fighter with the **Gargantuan** runemark (🐉) within 1" of this fighter and roll a number of dice equal to the value of this ability. For each 4+, subtract 1 from the Move characteristic of that fighter (to a minimum of 3) until the end of the battle.
	[Double] Dodge and Evade: Until the end of the battle round, add the value of this ability to the Toughness characteristic of this fighter when it is being targeted by an attack action made by a fighter with the **Gargantuan** runemark (🐉).
	[Double] Jump on its Back: Pick an enemy fighter with the **Gargantuan** runemark (🐉). Until the end of the battle round, if that fighter starts a move action within 1" of this fighter, then after that move action, you can remove this fighter from the battlefield and set them up within 1" of that fighter.
	[Triple] Go for the Eyes: If the next attack action made by this fighter this activation that targets an enemy fighter with the **Gargantuan** runemark (🐉) scores any critical hits, subtract 1 from the Attacks characteristic (to a minimum of 1) of attack actions made by that fighter until the end of the battle.
	[Triple] Gutting Strike: Add the value of this ability to the damage points allocated by each critical hit from attack actions made by this fighter this activation that have a Range characteristic of 3 or less and that target an enemy fighter with the **Gargantuan** runemark (🐉).
	[Quad] Taunt: Pick a visible enemy fighter with the **Gargantuan** runemark (🐉) that is within 6" of this fighter and roll a number of dice equal to the value of this ability. If a 4+ is rolled on any of the dice, then until the end of the battle round or until this fighter is taken down, attack actions made by that fighter must target this fighter.

MONSTER ABILITIES

	🐉	**[Double] Monstrous Reach:** Until the end of this fighter's activation, do not count the vertical distance when measuring the range for attack actions made by this fighter.
	🐉	**[Triple] Drag and Maul:** Pick a visible enemy fighter within 6" of this fighter. Remove that fighter from the battlefield and set them up within 1" of this fighter. Then, roll a number of dice equal to the value of this ability. For each 4+, allocate 3 damage points to that fighter.
	🐉	**[Quad] Demolishing Rampage:** Pick a terrain feature within 1" of this fighter. In an order of your choice, place each objective, treasure token and fighter that is on that terrain feature, and on any other terrain feature that is on that terrain feature, on the battlefield floor in a location of your choice as close as possible horizontally to its current location. Then, in an order of your choice, each fighter placed on the battlefield in this manner suffers impact damage. Then, remove the terrain feature(s).

USING MONSTERS IN YOUR BATTLES

Monsters can be used in games of Warcry in the following ways:

TWIST CARDS

Monsters with the **Chaotic Beasts** faction runemark (✱) can be used with any twist card that brings chaotic beasts into play.

INCLUDING MONSTERS IN YOUR WARBAND

Every monster in Warcry has one of the following faction runemarks:

- Chaotic Beasts (✱)
- Monsters of Order (⚡)
- Monsters of Death (⚡)
- Monsters of Destruction (⚡)

Chaos warbands can include monsters with the **Chaotic Beasts** faction runemark (✱). You can find the monsters with this faction runemark on the following pages.

Additionally, the rules for including a monster in your warband vary depending on the style of game you are playing:

OPEN PLAY

In open play, when mustering for a battle, you can include 1 monster in your warband. Monsters cost points just like any other fighter but are ignored for the purposes of the rule that requires all fighters in a warband to share the same faction runemark.

NARRATIVE PLAY

In narrative play, winning certain challenge battles will allow you to add a monster to your warband roster. In this book, the challenge battle 'Fury of the Wild' (pg 107) allows a Chaos warband to do so. You can find the rules for challenge battles on pages 104-105.

Your warband roster can include no more than 1 monster at any time. If you have the option to add a new monster to your warband roster and you wish to do so, you must first remove the existing monster from your warband roster.

Like other fighters, monsters can receive destiny levels and players must make injury rolls for them. However, monsters can never bear lesser artefacts or artefacts of power and can never be chosen to become favoured warriors.

When mustering for a campaign battle, you can include 1 monster from your warband roster in your warband. Monsters cost points just like any other fighter but are ignored for the purposes of the rule that requires all fighters in a warband to share the same faction runemark.

In addition, if you are playing a convergence, only the Aspirant player can include any monsters in their warband.

MATCHED PLAY

Monsters cannot be included in warbands in matched play battles. However, if both players agree, players should feel free to use the open play rules for monsters in their matched play games to allow them to include 1 monster in their warband.

CHIMERA

Born from the mutative caress of Chaos, a Chimera is an amalgamation of beasts – and all rage. From their many heads they spit flames and loose ear-splitting roars, and their sharp claws make short work of even the thickest armour.

DAMAGE TABLE

Damage Points Allocated	Move	Damage
0-10	12	5/10
11-20	10	4/8
21-30	8	3/6
31-40	6	2/4
41-50	4	1/2

CHIMERA ABILITIES

[Double] Tail Whip: Pick a visible enemy fighter within 3" of this fighter and roll a dice. On a 4-5, allocate 1 damage point to that fighter. On a 6, allocate a number of damage points to that fighter equal to the value of this ability.

[Triple] Leonine Roar: Until the end of the battle round, subtract 1 from the Attacks characteristic (to a minimum of 1) of attack actions made by enemy fighters while they are within 6" of this fighter.

[Quad] Draconic Head's Fiery Breath: Allocate a number of damage points equal to the value of this ability to all visible enemy fighters within 4" of this fighter.

 SLAUGHTERBRUTE

To witness a Slaughterbrute in battle is to see wrath given form. These raging beasts can only be controlled by ritual blades plunged into their spine – and should this leash slip, the violence that follows must be seen to be believed.

DAMAGE TABLE

Damage Points Allocated	Move	Damage
0-10	8	4/8
11-20	7	4/6
21-30	6	3/6
31-40	5	3/4
41-50	4	2/4

SLAUGHTERBRUTE ABILITIES

[Double] Mighty Jaws: Pick a visible enemy fighter within 1" of this fighter and roll a number of dice equal to the value of this ability. For each 3+, allocate 1 damage point to that fighter.

[Triple] Rampaging Charge: Until the end of this fighter's activation, the next time this fighter finishes a move action within 1" of an enemy fighter, pick a visible enemy fighter within 1" of this fighter. Allocate a number of damage points to that fighter equal to the value of this ability.

[Quad] Beast Unbound: This fighter makes a bonus attack action or a bonus move action.

 CHAOS GARGANT

Chaos Gargants are towering, ill-tempered brutes who have been warped by the touch of Chaos. More often than not thoroughly inebriated, their long limbs and mighty clubs have nevertheless spelt the doom for many a warband.

CHAOS GARGANT
315

🏹 ☀ 4 💀 50

DAMAGE TABLE

Damage Points Allocated	Move	Damage
0-10	6	4/8
11-20	5	4/6
21-30	4	3/6
31-40	3	3/4
41-50	2	2/4

CHAOS GARGANT ABILITIES

	[Double] Drunken Stagger: Roll a number of dice equal to the value of this ability. For each roll of 1-2, subtract 1 from this fighter's Move characteristic until the end of this fighter's activation. For each roll of 3+, add 1 to this fighter's Move characteristic until the end of this fighter's activation.
	[Triple] Mighty Kick: Until the end of this fighter's activation, the next time this fighter finishes a move action within 1" of an enemy fighter, pick a visible enemy fighter within 1" of this fighter. Allocate a number of damage points to that fighter equal to the value of this ability.
	[Quad] Vicious 'Eadbutt: Pick a visible enemy fighter within 1" of this fighter and roll a number of dice equal to the value of this ability. For each 4+, allocate a number of damage points to that fighter equal to the value of this ability.

GHORGON

Swollen with the cursed bloodgreed, Ghorgons eviscerate the foe with swings of their huge bladed limbs. Even in combat they are filled with an insatiable urge to feed, gulping down those warriors who present the tastiest morsels.

GHORGON
320

🏹 ☀ 4 💀 50

DAMAGE TABLE

Damage Points Allocated	Move	Damage
0-10	6	4/10
11-20	5	4/8
21-30	4	3/8
31-40	3	3/6
41-50	2	2/6

GHORGON ABILITIES

	[Double] Roaring Charge: Add half the value of this ability (rounding up) to the Move characteristic of this fighter for the next move action they make this activation.
	[Triple] Slavering Maw: Pick a visible enemy fighter within 1" of this fighter and roll a number of dice equal to the value of this ability. For each 3+, allocate 3 damage points to that fighter.
	[Quad] Ravenous Bloodgreed: This fighter can make a bonus move action a number of inches equal to the value of this ability. Then, this fighter can make a bonus attack action.

 CYGOR

A Cygor's single staring eye is attuned to the flow of magic. They hunger for the bright souls of spellcasters and others steeped in the power of sorcery, and with their huge strength can hurl chunks of masonry with great accuracy.

DAMAGE TABLE

DAMAGE POINTS ALLOCATED	MOVE	DAMAGE
0-10	6	4/8
11-20	5	4/6
21-30	4	3/6
31-40	3	3/4
41-50	2	2/4

CYGOR ABILITIES

[Double] Rip and Tear Masonry: This fighter can use this ability only if they are within 1" of an obstacle. If this fighter is empty-handed (see below), they are no longer empty-handed.

[Triple] Hurl Boulder: This fighter can use this ability only if they are not empty-handed (see below). Pick a visible enemy fighter within 15" of this fighter and roll a number of dice equal to the value of this ability. For each roll of 4+, allocate 5 damage points to that fighter. After using this ability, this fighter is said to be *empty-handed*.

[Quad] Soul-eater: Roll a dice for each enemy fighter within 6" of this fighter. On a 4+, allocate 3 damage points to the fighter being rolled for and remove 3 damage points from this fighter.

 MUTALITH VORTEX BEAST

Few creatures are more bizarre or more terrifying than a Mutalith Vortex Beast. These tentacled abominations are capable of opening a gateway directly to the Realm of Chaos, subjecting those nearby to waves of mutative power.

DAMAGE TABLE

DAMAGE POINTS ALLOCATED	MOVE	DAMAGE
0-10	8	4/8
11-20	7	4/6
21-30	6	3/6
31-40	5	3/4
41-50	4	2/4

MUTALITH VORTEX BEAST ABILITIES

[Double] Maw Tentacles: Pick a visible enemy fighter within 6" of this fighter. That enemy fighter makes a bonus move action directly towards this fighter, as if they were jumping, a number of inches equal to the value of this ability. When doing so, they can move away from enemy fighters within 1" at the start of that move action.

[Triple] Mutant Regeneration: Roll a number of dice equal to the value of this ability. For each 4+, remove 3 damage points allocated to this fighter.

[Quad] Aura of Mutation: Allocate a number of damage points equal to half the value of this ability (rounding up) to all visible enemy fighters within 3" of this fighter. In addition, roll a dice for each visible enemy fighter within 3" of this fighter. On a 6, that fighter cannot activate this battle round.

HELL PIT
ABOMINATION

The deranged masterworks of the Clans Moulder, Hell Pit Abominations are fleshmelded monstrosities of dreadful power. Even to slay such a monster carries with it great risk, for tides of rabid vermin spill forth from rents in their flesh.

HELL PIT ABOMINATION · 305 · 2 · 5 · 4 · / · 55

HELL PIT ABOMINATION ABILITIES

		[Double] Regenerating Monstrosity: Roll a number of dice equal to the value of this ability. For each 4+, remove 3 damage points allocated to this fighter.
		[Triple] Avalanche of Flesh: Until the end of this fighter's activation, the next time this fighter finishes a move action within 1" of an enemy fighter, pick a visible enemy fighter within 1" of this fighter. Allocate a number of damage points to that fighter equal to the value of this ability.
		[Quad] Too Horrible to Die: Until the end of the battle round, after each attack action with a Range characteristic of 3 or less that targets this fighter, roll 3 dice. For each 5+, allocate 3 damage points to the fighter that made the attack action.

DAMAGE TABLE

DAMAGE POINTS ALLOCATED	MOVE	DAMAGE
0-10	6	4/10
11-20	5	4/8
21-30	4	3/8
31-40	3	3/6
41-54	2	2/6

 CHAOS THRALLS

All manner of slavering pack-beasts and mutated horrors can be found across the Bloodwind Spoil. Whether striking from ambush or swarming in vast numbers, they are deadly opponents capable of slaughtering a host of the unwary.

CHAOTIC BEASTS ABILITIES

		[Triple] Cower: Until the end of the battle round, count each critical hit from attack actions that target this fighter as a hit instead.
		[Triple] Crazed Flock: Until the end of this fighter's activation, for each other friendly fighter within 3" of this fighter that has the same runemarks as this fighter, add 1 to the Attacks and Strength characteristics of attack actions made by this fighter that have a Range characteristic of 3 or less.
		[Double] Outrunner of Chaos: Add half the value of this ability (rounding up) to the Move characteristic of this fighter for the next move action they make this activation.
		[Triple] Writhing Tentacles: Add the value of this ability to the Attacks characteristic of the next attack action made by this fighter this activation that has a Range characteristic of 3 or less.
		[Triple] Uncontrollable Stampede: Until the end of this fighter's activation, the next time this fighter finishes a move action within 1" of an enemy fighter, pick an enemy fighter within 1" of this fighter. Allocate a number of damage points to that fighter equal to the value of this ability.

WARBANDS OF CHAOS

In this section, you will find updated rules for Warcry warbands dedicated to the Dark Gods of Chaos. Detailed background will reveal the secrets of these damned hosts and their ultimate plans for dominance within the Bloodwind Spoil. Also included is a complete list of fighter cards for every warrior and hero available to Chaos warbands, designed to be easy to navigate and reference even in the midst of the most nail-biting skirmish battles.

Each warband also has access to a range of unique abilities specially tailored for them, representing the powers, skills and sorceries they employ to triumph over their foes and stay alive in the deadly Bloodwind Spoil.

'Death to Sigmar! Death to the craven God-King! Glory to the Dark Gods beyond the veil!'

BEASTS OF CHAOS

In the warped wilds of the Mortal Realms, the Beasts of Chaos lurk. These rampaging despoilers loathe with a furious intensity all that is civilised, and when riled into a frenzy they attack with relentless savagery.

The Beasts of Chaos consider themselves to be the true children of ruin. Each is a hideous amalgamation of man, animal and pure anarchy, bound together in obscene form by the warping energies of Chaos. Yet unlike most servants of the Dark Gods, who only became widespread during the Age of Chaos, the beast-kin have dwelt in the Mortal Realms since long before the coming of the God-King. Though their primitive warbands were forced to the margins of existence by the upstart forces of civilisation, they were never truly defeated. Now, even as the Age of Sigmar challenges the dominion of Chaos, they spill forth from the darkest corners of the realms to savage any who would dare settle their ancestral hunting grounds.

The Beasts of Chaos prize only those deeds that are truest to their base natures. To crush, to despoil, to slaughter and cast down; these

are the acts that grant prestige and authority amongst the beastherds, for these are the ways by which the children of Chaos revel in their primal strength. They despise the ordered hosts of the undead and the technological innovations of Sigmar's cities, for these are seen as perversions of the anarchic truths of existence. Even the riotous hordes of Destruction have earned the seething fury of the beast-kin, as battle purely for its own sake cannot sate the hatred of all that is structured and civil that burns in their malevolent hearts.

Even the warriors of the Dark Gods are not safe from the ravages of the beast-kin; though they look upon the anarchy wrought by the Ruinous Powers with awe, they also despise those who would sell their souls to any higher entity for greater power. This antipathy even extends to looking down upon daemons as being enslaved to their

creators; for the Beasts of Chaos, the only true measure of strength is that which can be demonstrated in raw and direct fashion. Though there are those who have been claimed by a single dark power, it is a comparative rarity when judged against most mortal devotees of Chaos. The beastmen are ruin in its truest form, furious and primal, and were they to have their way even the gods themselves would devolve into an all-consuming vortex of sheer anarchy.

The most prolific Beasts of Chaos are known as gor-kin. Though their form may, and often does, vary, the majority have animalistic features, thick manes of unkempt fur that bristle across their leathery hides and sharp, jutting horns. These horns are considered a prominent status symbol amongst the gor-kin; the lowliest amongst their number, known as Ungors, possess only rudimentary buds of bone, while

'true' Gors and the savage chieftains who lead them will be blessed with great, twisting crowns of the osseous material. The warriors of these brayherds are not great tacticians, nor are they graceful or elegant fighters, but only a fool would underestimate them. Their every blow is driven by such fury that they can cleave straight through armour. They are capable of shrugging off terrible wounds, and can run down their prey with shocking swiftness. Perhaps the most dangerous trait of the gor-kin, however, is their animalistic cunning. They are masters of the ambush, lying in wait with a predator's patience before erupting from cover and overwhelming the foe in a storm of blades and horns.

Other, stranger creatures make war alongside the gor-kin. Towering, blood-hungry Bullgors provide terrible might to the brayherds; each of these beasts stands as tall and broad as an ogor, and their ravenous hunger for warm, succulent flesh renders them capable of truly savage violence. From the most twisted regions of the realms emerge flocks of trilling Tzeentchian beast-kin and mewling Chaos Spawn, while drunken Centigors and snarling hounds chase down any who seek to flee the beastherds. Perhaps most terrible are the Dragon Ogors. Ancient denizens of Azyr cast out by Sigmar, these beings view all the God-King's works with utter loathing, and delight in any opportunity to take revenge upon his people.

'The storm god's spawn build such pretty walls. They shoot their fire-sticks and hurl their sky-magic; they bang their drums and wave their flags.

But Gor has axe. Gor has horns. Gor has hate. We see which is better, in the end.'

- Kharzugarn, Beastlord of
the Gorehorns Greatfray

Ever since the dark days of the Nexus Wars, where the legions of Archaon remade the Allpoints in their own twisted image, the Beasts of Chaos have claimed swathes of the continent sub-realm as their hunting lands. Savage bands known as Wild Stalkers roam freely there, for the laws of the Eightpoints – that the strong survive, the weak perish and the land itself languishes in a constant state of rebellious flux – appeals to the hateful creed of the beast-kin. The mountain range known as the Fangs, situated near the heart of the Bloodwind Spoil, is particularly infamous for the number of beastmen who haunt its shadowy ravines. Its crevasses and overhangs are marked by the stacked bones and flayed flesh of former interlopers, arrayed around hideous Herdstones that leer from the shadows. To trespass in those lands invites painful death, whether it comes through frenzied dismemberment, exposure to the warping powers of Chaos or being sacrificed in the foul bacchanals led by the Bray-Shaman leaders of the tribes.

Carngrad has been attacked many times by beastmen warbands; though the city is a ramshackle and fluctuating thing, even the merest hint of civilisation is sufficient to drive the denizens of the warped wilds into a frenzy. Unlike some warbands, the Beasts of Chaos do not typically seek out esoteric artefacts or forgotten lore, for such things have little to offer a breed of creatures that respect only strength. Still, the chance to desecrate such prizes – or simply to deny them to those who would seek to enhance themselves with borrowed power – can be a tempting proposition for cunning Bray-Shamans and Beastlords. Should the Beasts of Chaos succeed in their savage aims, then the Eightpoints will descend into utter anarchy and primal madness – so much so that even the gods themselves may keep their distance, or risk ending up as prey.

BEASTS OF CHAOS

The greatest strength of the Beasts of Chaos is their raw, animalistic savagery. Whether striking from cunningly prepared ambushes or overwhelming their foes through sheer brute strength, these bestial monstrosities tear apart their hated foes with unbridled ferocity.

BEASTS OF CHAOS FIGHTER ABILITIES

	[Double] Brayherd Ambush: A fighter can use this ability only if it is the first battle round. This fighter can make a bonus move action of a number of inches equal to the value of this ability.
	[Double] Bloodgorge: A fighter can use this ability only if an enemy fighter has been taken down by an attack action made by them this activation. Remove a number of damage points allocated to this fighter equal to the value of this ability.
	[Triple] Petrifying Gaze: Pick 1 visible enemy fighter within 8" of this fighter and roll a dice. On a 2+, allocate a number of damage points to that fighter equal to the roll. In addition, subtract 1 from the Move characteristic (to a minimum of 1) of that fighter until the end of the battle round.
	[Triple] Bestial Charge: Until the end of this fighter's activation, the next time this fighter finishes a move action within 1" of an enemy fighter, pick a visible enemy fighter within 1" of this fighter. Allocate a number of damage points to that fighter equal to the value of this ability.
	[Triple] Volley of Arrows: Add half the value of this ability (rounding up) to the Attacks characteristic of the next attack action made by this fighter this activation that targets an enemy fighter more than 3" away.
	[Quad] Bring Down the Storm: Pick 1 visible enemy fighter within 20" of this fighter and roll 1 dice. On a 2+, allocate a number of damage points to that fighter equal to the value of this ability.

BEASTS OF CHAOS LEADER ABILITIES

	[Double] Rip, Gore and Tear!: A fighter can use this ability only if an enemy fighter has been taken down by an attack action made by them this activation. This fighter makes a bonus move action or a bonus attack action.
	[Double] Devolve: Pick a visible enemy fighter within 6" of this fighter. That fighter makes a bonus move action directly towards this fighter, as if they were jumping, a number of inches equal to the value of this ability.
	[Triple] Grisly Trophy: A fighter can use this ability only if an enemy fighter has been taken down by an attack action made by them this activation. Until the end of the battle round, add 1 to the Attacks characteristic of attack actions that have a Range characteristic of 3 or less made by visible friendly fighters while they are within 9" of this fighter.
	[Quad] Empowering Lightning: For each friendly fighter with the **Beasts of Chaos** (🐂) and **Destroyer** (🐙) runemarks within 9" of this fighter, you can remove a number of damage points allocated to that fighter equal to the value of this ability.

GREAT BRAY-SHAMAN — 195

UNGOR RAIDER HALFHORN — 140

BEASTLORD — 200

GOUGE-HORN — 185

DOOMBULL — 265

BLOODKINE WITH PAIRED BULLGOR AXES — 245

DRAGON OGOR SHAGGOTH — 255

BLOODKINE WITH BULLGOR GREAT AXE — 250

FOE-RENDER — 170

BLOODKINE WITH BULLGOR AXE AND BULLSHIELD — 240

UNGOR HALFHORN — 130

GOREHOOF — 205

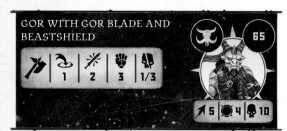

GOR WITH GOR BLADE AND BEASTSHIELD

65

⚔	1	2	3	1/3

5 | 4 | 10

UNGOR WITH UNGOR BLADE AND HALF-SHIELD

60

	1	2	3	1/3

5 | 4 | 8

GOR WITH PAIR OF GOR BLADES

55

⚔	1	3	3	1/3

5 | 3 | 10

UNGOR RAIDER

70

	3-15	2	3	1/3
	1	2	3	1/3

5 | 3 | 8

UNGOR WITH GNARLED SHORTSPEAR AND HALF-SHIELD

70

	2	2	3	1/4

5 | 4 | 8

BESTIGOR

115

⚔	1	3	4	2/4

5 | 4 | 12

DRAGON OGOR WITH PAIRED ANCIENT WEAPONS — 195

⚒		✳	✊	🛡
1	5	4	2/4	

➵ 6 | ☀ 4 | 💀 30

DRAGON OGOR WITH DRACONIC WAR-GLAIVE — 195

⟡		✳	✊	🛡
2	4	4	2/5	

➵ 6 | ☀ 4 | 💀 30

DRAGON OGOR WITH DRACONIC CRUSHER — 195

⚒		✳	✊	🛡
1	3	4	3/6	

➵ 6 | ☀ 4 | 💀 30

BULLGOR WITH PAIRED BULLGOR AXES — 190

⚒		✳	✊	🛡
1	4	5	2/4	

➵ 5 | ☀ 4 | 💀 30

BULLGOR WITH BULLGOR GREAT AXE — 190

⚒		✳	✊	🛡
1	2	5	3/6	

➵ 5 | ☀ 4 | 💀 30

BULLGOR WITH BULLGOR AXE AND BULLSHIELD — 190

⚒		✳	✊	🛡
1	3	5	2/4	

➵ 5 | ☀ 5 | 💀 30

CENTIGOR — 135

⟡		✳	✊	🛡
2	2	4	1/4	

➵ 10 | ☀ 4 | 💀 18

COCKATRICE — 210

⟡		✳	✊	🛡
1	4	4	2/5	

➵ 10 | ☀ 4 | 💀 30

BLADES OF KHORNE

Across the Mortal Realms, the warriors of Khorne plunge into furious battle. There is no mercy to be found in their savage hearts, for they know that their god cares not from where the blood flows – only that it does.

The entity known to mortalkind as Khorne is considered by many seers and scholars to be the eldest of the Chaos Gods, and possibly the most powerful. A gestalt manifestation of hate and fury, it is unsurprising that Khorne is typically honoured as a god of the most brutal, uncompromising breed of warfare. From atop a mountainous throne of skulls the Blood God watches countless armies battle across all of creation, bellowing in wrathful appreciation for each life taken and river of gore spilt.

Khorne's influence – or perhaps more accurately, the intense wrathful emotions that initially birthed the god – is indelibly scarred onto the minds of mortals. Amidst the darkness and horror of the realms, where each day can be a struggle simply to survive, it is perhaps unsurprising that many would be drawn into the worship of the lord of battle in return for strength in war; even Sigmar's cities play host to hidden blood-cults and secret warrior-fraternities dedicated to Khorne, no matter how hard the Lord-Veritants attempt to root them out. While some Chaos-tainted cultures venerate Khorne as a somewhat honourable patron of soldiers or an atavistic hunter-lord bedecked in the skulls of slaughtered beasts, most believe the Blood God to be a bringer of slaughter and granter of battle rage, an unstoppable elemental force that seeks nothing more than to turn the material plane into one endless battleground.

There was a time when Khorne reigned supreme over much of the Mortal Realms. As the Age of Chaos reached its height, the warriors of the Blood God had put countless lands to the sword; Aqshy in particular had suffered under their blades, for the volatile passions that ruled this realm have ever appealed to Khorne's rage. Even the worshippers of the other Dark Gods were not safe, for the Lord of Skulls will suffer no rivals. A hateful enmity has long existed between Khorne and Slaanesh, but the pustulent children of Nurgle and scheming sorcerers of Tzeentch were dragged from their fortresses and messily slaughtered all the same.

'Blood for the Blood God! Skulls for the Skull Throne!'

- Battle cry of countless warriors lost to Khorne's rage

If this Red Century represented the apogee of Khorne's power, however, then the resurgence of Order and return of civilisation to the Mortal Realms – limited as it is – has proven quite the opposite. Yet the Blood God only grows stronger upon conflict. Striking from the bone-strewn plains and badlands, the marauding tribes

and hordes sworn to Khorne remain a constant threat to the nascent free cities. Given the chance they will drown Sigmar's burgeoning empire in a wave of gore, and turn each city into a charnel altar of spilt blood and stacked skulls.

Khorne's favoured mortal servants are known as the Bloodbound. Whether they were born into tribes that venerate battle and slaughter, or were once considered civilised but devoted themselves to the Lord of Skulls in return for the power to conquer their enemies, these men and women have been utterly consumed by the lust for carnage that typifies their wrathful deity. Their armies comprise cannibalistic Bloodreavers led by raging demagogues and mighty champions of battle. Savage Blood Warriors, chosen devotees of Khorne who have undergone the dreaded Red Baptism, provide the forces of the Bloodbound with elite armoured troops. They are joined in their furious rages by a host of unnatural beings, from the half-daemonic Wrathmongers – whose sheer presence inspires a berserk fury in their allies – to the frenzied Skullreapers and hideous mutant warbeasts known as Khorgoraths.

Should the Bloodbound perform enough acts of slaughter to thin the walls of reality, the Blood God's daemons may be drawn forth to claim their own tally of skulls. Each of these beings was born in the heart of Khorne's rage, a splinter of their god that cares only for mindless carnage. Bloodletters form the heart of these daemonic armies, their wicked hellblades dripping with gore and their eyes alight with the need to slay. Loping alongside them are packs of vicious Flesh Hounds, tireless hunters dedicated to pursuing those mortals who earn Khorne's targeted ire. Bloodcrushers, meanwhile, are daemonic shock cavalry who ride atop clanking brutes known as Juggernauts, and who can smash aside the stoutest shieldwall in a single furious charge.

The Eightpoints have been the site of furious battle for centuries, and thus it is no surprise that the followers of Khorne can be found in abundance there. Unlike many other warbands, be they dedicated to the Dark Gods or otherwise, these blood-mad killers rarely travel to the lands of the Varanspire with any particular purpose in mind; the call of simple, unending war is sufficient in itself. The Wrathbands of the Bloodbound build no permanent encampments, and even those monoliths raised to their god's glory are little more than heaped piles of flayed skulls and shattered bone. Theirs is a nomadic existence punctuated by intermittent bouts of blood-drenched, close-quarters carnage.

On those occasions that a Khornate warband is charged with a specific purpose, it is often some form of hunt. The Blood God despises cowardice in all its forms – particularly the use of magic, which Khorne sees as the wielding of power that has not been earned – and thus many of the god's red-handed champions and daemonic warbands known as Bloodseekers strive to run such marked individuals to the ground. Through claiming their skulls, they earn the favour of their bloodthirsty deity. Yet these are not the only hunts Khorne's faithful engage in. From tracking down relic weaponry to claiming sacrifices, the Blades of Khorne are a relentless scourge on the Bloodwind Spoil.

KHORNE BLOODBOUND

The cannibal warriors of the Bloodbound crash into the foe like an unstoppable, gore-streaked axe blade. From lightly armoured but ferocious Bloodreavers to mutated Skullreapers and hulking Slaughterpriests, their numberless battle-hungry warriors are the bane of civilisation.

KHORNE BLOODBOUND FIGHTER ABILITIES

[Double] Blood for the Blood God: A fighter can use this ability only if an enemy fighter has been taken down by an attack action made by them this activation. This fighter makes a bonus move action or a bonus attack action.

[Double] Gorefist: Pick a visible enemy fighter within 1" of this fighter and roll a dice. On a 3-4, allocate 1 damage point to that fighter. On a 5-6, allocate a number of damage points to that fighter equal to the value of this ability.

[Double] Lashing Bone Tentacles: Pick a visible enemy fighter within 6" of this fighter and roll 2 dice. For each 4-5, allocate 1 damage point to that fighter. For each 6, allocate a number of damage points to that fighter equal to the value of this ability.

[Triple] Murderous Charge: Until the end of this fighter's activation, the next time this fighter finishes a move action within 1" of an enemy fighter, pick a visible enemy fighter within 1" of this fighter. Allocate a number of damage points to that fighter equal to the value of this ability.

[Triple] Daemon-forged Weapons: Until the end of this fighter's activation, add half the value of this ability (rounding up) to each critical hit scored by attack actions made by this fighter that have a Range characteristic of 3 or less.

[Quad] Blood-fuelled Assault: This fighter makes a bonus move action. Then, they can make a bonus attack action. In addition, until the end of this fighter's activation, add half the value of this ability (rounding up) to the Strength characteristic of attack actions made by this fighter that have a Range characteristic of 3 or less.

KHORNE BLOODBOUND LEADER ABILITIES

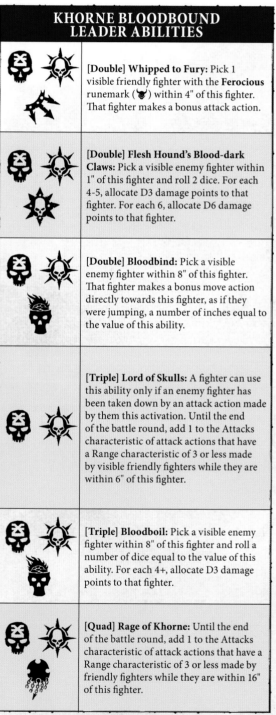

[Double] Whipped to Fury: Pick 1 visible friendly fighter with the **Ferocious** runemark (☖) within 4" of this fighter. That fighter makes a bonus attack action.

[Double] Flesh Hound's Blood-dark Claws: Pick a visible enemy fighter within 1" of this fighter and roll 2 dice. For each 4-5, allocate D3 damage points to that fighter. For each 6, allocate D6 damage points to that fighter.

[Double] Bloodbind: Pick a visible enemy fighter within 8" of this fighter. That fighter makes a bonus move action directly towards this fighter, as if they were jumping, a number of inches equal to the value of this ability.

[Triple] Lord of Skulls: A fighter can use this ability only if an enemy fighter has been taken down by an attack action made by them this activation. Until the end of the battle round, add 1 to the Attacks characteristic of attack actions that have a Range characteristic of 3 or less made by visible friendly fighters while they are within 6" of this fighter.

[Triple] Bloodboil: Pick a visible enemy fighter within 8" of this fighter and roll a number of dice equal to the value of this ability. For each 4+, allocate D3 damage points to that fighter.

[Quad] Rage of Khorne: Until the end of the battle round, add 1 to the Attacks characteristic of attack actions that have a Range characteristic of 3 or less made by friendly fighters while they are within 16" of this fighter.

KHORNE BLOODBOUND WRATHBANDS

ASPIRING DEATHBRINGER

210

	1	4	4	2/4

4 | 5 | 30

SLAUGHTERPRIEST WITH BLOODBATHED AXE

210

	1	3	4	3/5

4 | 4 | 32

EXALTED DEATHBRINGER WITH IMPALING SPEAR

205

	2	3	4	3/6

4 | 4 | 30

SLAUGHTERPRIEST WITH WRATH-HAMMER AND HACKBLADE

210

	1	4	4	2/4
	3	3	4	1/4

4 | 4 | 32

EXALTED DEATHBRINGER WITH RUINOUS AXE

205

	1	4	4	3/5

4 | 4 | 30

BLOODSECRATOR

210

	1	3	4	2/5

4 | 5 | 30

SKULLGRINDER

230

	2	2	5	3/6

4 | 5 | 30

MIGHTY LORD OF KHORNE

240

	1	5	4	2/5

4 | 5 | 32

MIGHTY LORD OF KHORNE ON JUGGERNAUT
280

	1	4	4	2/5

6 · 6 · 38

SKULLSEEKER
195

	1	4	4	2/4

4 · 4 · 30

BLOODSTOKER
200

	3	3	4	1/4
	1	4	4	2/4

4 · 4 · 30

CHAOS CHAMPION
185

	1	4	4	2/4

4 · 4 · 25

SKULLHUNTER
265

	1	4	4	2/4

6 · 6 · 35

BLOODREAVER CHIEFTAIN
140

	1	5	3	2/4

5 · 3 · 20

WRATHMASTER
210

	2	6	4	2/4

4 · 4 · 30

BLOODREAVER WITH REAVER BLADES
65

1	4	3	1/3

5 | 3 | 10

WRATHMONGER
170

2	5	4	1/4

4 | 4 | 25

BLOODREAVER WITH MEATRIPPER AXE
65

1	3	4	1/3

5 | 3 | 10

KHORGORATH
235

1	3	5	4/8

4 | 4 | 35

BLOOD WARRIOR WITH GOREAXE AND GOREFIST
110

1	3	3	2/4

4 | 4 | 15

MIGHTY SKULLCRUSHER WITH ENSORCELLED AXE
220

1	3	4	2/4

6 | 6 | 30

BLOOD WARRIOR WITH PAIR OF GOREAXES
115

1	4	3	2/4

4 | 4 | 15

MIGHTY SKULLCRUSHER WITH BLOODGLAIVE
225

2	2	5	2/4

6 | 6 | 30

BLOOD WARRIOR WITH GOREGLAIVE
120

1	3	4	2/5

4 | 4 | 15

FLESH HOUND
170

1	4	4	2/4

8 | 4 | 20

SKULLREAPER
165

1	4	4	2/4

4 | 4 | 25

DAEMONS OF KHORNE

Wherever the slaughter is greatest, the Daemons of Khorne tread. These gore-soaked beings are given form by mortal rage and the will of their dread master, and care for nothing beyond the taking of life and the claiming of skulls – all to ensure the blood flows eternally.

DAEMONS OF KHORNE ABILITIES	
	[Double] Blood for the Blood God: A fighter can use this ability only if an enemy fighter has been taken down by an attack action made by them this activation. This fighter makes a bonus move action or a bonus attack action.
	[Double] Decapitating Strike: Add half the value of this ability (rounding up) to the number of damage points allocated by critical hits from the next attack action made by this fighter this activation that has a Range characteristic of 3 or less.
	[Double] Hungry for Flesh: A fighter can use this ability only if there is a visible enemy fighter within 6" of them. This fighter makes a bonus move action and must finish closer to the closest visible enemy fighter than they were at the start of that move action.
	[Triple] Locus of Fury: A fighter can use this ability only if an enemy fighter has been taken down by an attack action made by them this activation. Until the end of the battle round, add 1 to the Attacks characteristic of attack actions that have a Range characteristic of 3 or less made by visible friendly fighters while they are within 6" of this fighter.
	[Triple] Murderous Charge: Until the end of this fighter's activation, the next time this fighter finishes a move action within 1" of an enemy fighter, pick a visible enemy fighter within 1" of this fighter. Allocate a number of damage points to that fighter equal to the value of this ability.
	[Quad] Burning Roar: Pick a visible enemy fighter within 8" of this fighter and roll a number of dice equal to the value of this ability. For each 2+, allocate 2 damage points to that fighter.

DAEMONS OF KHORNE BLOODSEEKERS

SKULLMASTER, HERALD OF KHORNE
265

⚔	�’	✳	✊	🛡
1	5	4	2/5	

➹ 6 | ☀ 5 | 💀 38

BLOODLETTER
70

⚔	�’	✳	✊	🛡
1	4	3	1/4	

➹ 4 | ☀ 3 | 💀 10

BLOODMASTER, HERALD OF KHORNE
190

⚔	�’	✳	✊	🛡
1	5	4	2/5	

➹ 4 | ☀ 4 | 💀 22

FLESH HOUND
170

🦷	�’	✳	✊	🛡
1	4	4	2/4	

➹ 8 | ☀ 4 | 💀 20

BLOODREAPER
150

⚔	�’	✳	✊	🛡
1	5	4	2/4	

➹ 4 | ☀ 3 | 💀 20

GORE HOUND
205

🦷	�’	✳	✊	🛡
1	5	4	2/5	

➹ 8 | ☀ 4 | 💀 25

BLOODHUNTER
240

⚔	�’	✳	✊	🛡
1	5	4	2/5	

➹ 6 | ☀ 4 | 💀 35

BLOODCRUSHER
185

⚔	�’	✳	✊	🛡
1	4	4	2/4	

➹ 6 | ☀ 4 | 💀 30

DISCIPLES OF TZEENTCH

The Disciples of Tzeentch triumph over their enemies through arcane might, patient cunning and sheer unpredictability. Their labyrinthine plots have brought misery and ruin to countless civilisations.

Of all the Chaos Gods, it is perhaps Tzeentch who is worshipped in the greatest number of guises. Known as the Changer of the Ways, the Architect of Fate, the Lord of Flux and Tchar the Burning Eagle, Tzeentch attracts those mortals who desire knowledge and power. In truth, Tzeentch's sphere is hope, but of the most sinister and corrupting kind. Through whispering in the ears of those who seek to better their lot and rise above their station, this mad god traps the unwary in gossamer webs of anarchy and impossibly complex schemes.

The Architect of Fate favours those possessed of guile, creativity and ruthless ambition. Many revolutionaries and rabble-rousers unintentionally dance to Tzeentch's demented tune, and those who pay homage to this Chaos power find themselves aptly rewarded. Of all the dark pantheon, Tzeentch is the greatest patron of sorcery, for magic is amongst the most potent drivers of change in the cosmos; even the lowliest of those who serve the Lord of Flux are blessed with a measure of arcane skill, while the greatest possess power that would take a magister of the Collegiate Arcane decades of diligent study to achieve.

'Gates might bar your fortresses, but what guards your mind?'

- Yg'Rixirak, Eater of Ironies

Yet as with everything that stems from the Ruinous Powers, there is inevitably a price to pay for these boons. Tzeentch's essence is fundamentally transmogrifying in nature, the mortal aspirations and desire for change that gave birth to the god also bestowing the Architect of Fate with great power over mutation. Those who receive too much of his divine attention are liable to end their days as a mound of writhing flesh. Of course, the minds of such devotees are often so twisted by this point that they consider this just another gift. More sinister is the fact that Tzeentch's plots are often fundamentally self-defeating. They are schemes for the sake of schemes, and those champions of Change who perceived themselves to be high in their master's favour may suddenly find that they were nothing more than an expendable pawn all along.

The rise of Sigmar's cities has served Tzeentch's schemes well. Such urban settlements are inevitably hotbeds of intrigue and scheming,

and there are many politicians and merchants willing to cry out to the darkness to secure success in their endeavours. In the shadows of civilisation, Arcanite cults filled with sorcerous Kairic Acolytes plot the downfall of the mighty. In daily life these individuals cloak themselves in illusion, playing the roles of unassuming scribes, students and so on. Only when the call to rise up is given do they dispel these glamours and reveal their true powers. This call is inevitably sounded by the Magisters, twisted warlocks blessed the Changer of the Ways and granted great command of the arcane arts. They are the leaders of the Arcanite cults, tugging at the strings of fate to serve their own ends. Other, stranger creatures and champions can be found amongst the mortal hosts of Tzeentch. From mist-shrouded forests emerge flocks of Tzaangors, guided by their shamans in pursuit of their god's inscrutable will. Curselings and Ogroid Thaumaturges are just some examples of the champions that associate with the Arcanite cults, all to serve the greater aims of Tzeentch.

When the necessary rituals of summoning are performed and the power of change waxes across the realms, Tzeentch's gibbering daemons spill forth from the Crystal Labyrinth. Of all the spawn of the Dark Gods, these are perhaps the most bizarre in form and deed. From swooping sky-sharks and self-duplicating Horrors to bounding, fire-spewing Flamers, they are an assault on all that is reasoned and sane. Many of Tzeentch's daemons are spellcasters, or at least possessed of some affinity with warpflame. This scintillating fire does not burn and consume as a typical blaze does, but instead breeds rampant mutation and madness in whatever it touches, bringing the Mortal Realms closer to Tzeentch's vision of a reality locked in a state of constant flux.

Tzeentch has long coveted the realm of Chamon, for its alchemical properties render it highly susceptible to change-magics. As such, the Bloodwind Spoil – situated as it is in close proximity to the Chamonic arcway – is populated by many of the Great Manipulator's servants. Tzaangor flocks regularly battle against other bestial warbands for dominion of the Fangs mountain range, or otherwise roam far and wide across the tortured land raising flux-cairns and carrying out the will of their strange shamans. In the shadows of Carngrad gatherings of Tzeentchian cultists plot and scheme to pit the ruling Talons against one another – and, of course, to increase their own standing and satisfy their boundless ambition amidst the ensuing violence and confusion.

Arcanite Covens claim abandoned towers throughout the wastes as their own, working dark experiments on hoarded realmstone away from prying eyes. Even champions who have not pledged themselves directly to Tzeentch may find themselves drawn into the schemes of these warbands, their fortunes rising or falling in line with the meddling of the Great Manipulator's servants.

Tzeentch's daemons are almost impossible to anticipate, often because they themselves are content merely to follow their own whims and those of their fickle master. Roving Fatetwister Bands of these demented creatures ebb and flow across the Bloodwind Spoil, often engaged in some treacherous and unknowable endeavour that sees them harness the corrupting magics which constantly scour the lands of the Eightpoints. Tales are told around tribal campfires of the ravages of Tzeentch's spawn, and the perils of forming pacts with them. Some of the most cunning – or most insane – lords of the Eightpoints have managed to deal with these capricious creatures, but always they must keep a weather eye out for deceit, for the children of the Great Manipulator are as malicious as they are hideously imaginative.

TZEENTCH ARCANITES

The Arcanite cabals lurk in the shadow of civilisation, weaving sinister plots and twisting the strands of fate to their own ends. Throngs of sorcerous cultists fight alongside trilling beastkin and mutated mortal champions, stoking the flames of change through their arcane mastery.

TZEENTCH ARCANITES FIGHTER ABILITIES	
	[Double] Uttered Words of Arcane Power: Add 1 to the Attacks and Strength characteristics of the next attack action made by this fighter this activation that has a Range characteristic of 3 or less.
	[Double] Vulcharc: Pick an enemy fighter within 20" of this fighter. Until the end of the battle round, that fighter cannot make disengage actions.
	[Double] Vicious Beak: Pick a visible enemy fighter within 1" of this fighter and roll a number of dice equal to the value of this ability. For each 4+, allocate 1 damage point to that fighter.
	[Triple] Guided by the Past: Add half the value of this ability (rounding up) to the damage points allocated by each hit or critical hit from the next attack action made by this fighter this activation that has a Range characteristic of 3 or less and that targets an enemy fighter that has activated this battle round.
	[Quad] Guided by the Future: Add half the value of this ability (rounding up) to the damage points allocated by each hit or critical hit from the next attack action made by this fighter this activation that targets an enemy fighter that has not activated this battle round.

TZEENTCH ARCANITES LEADER ABILITIES	
	[Double] Locus of Sorcery: Add half the value of this ability (rounding up) to the Strength characteristic of the next attack action made by this fighter this activation that targets an enemy fighter more than 3" away.
	[Double] Brutal Rage: A fighter can use this ability only if 15 or more damage points have been allocated to them. Until the end of the battle, add 1 to the Attacks characteristic of attack actions made by this fighter that have a Range characteristic of 3 or less.
	[Triple] Master of Destiny: Until the end of the battle round, add the value of this ability to the value of other abilities (to a maximum of 6) used by friendly fighters within 12" of this fighter.
	[Triple] Warptongue Blade: Pick a visible enemy fighter within 1" of this fighter and roll a number of dice equal to the value of this ability. On a 2-5, allocate 1 damage point to that fighter. On a 6, allocate 3 damage points to that fighter.
	[Triple] Lord of Fate: Until the end of the battle round, add 1 to the Attacks characteristic of attack actions that have a Range characteristic of 3 or less made by friendly fighters while they are within 9" of this fighter.

TZEENTCH ARCANITE COVENS

MAGISTER ON DISC OF TZEENTCH
285

| | 3-10 | 2 | 3 | 3/6 |
| | 1 | 4 | 4 | 2/4 |

10 · 4 · 25

GAUNT SUMMONER OF TZEENTCH ON DISC
295

| | 3-10 | 2 | 3 | 3/6 |
| | 1 | 4 | 4 | 2/4 |

10 · 4 · 28

MAGISTER
190

| | 3-10 | 2 | 3 | 3/6 |
| | 1 | 3 | 4 | 1/4 |

4 · 3 · 22

GAUNT SUMMONER OF TZEENTCH
195

| | 3-10 | 2 | 3 | 3/6 |
| | 1 | 3 | 4 | 1/4 |

4 · 3 · 22

TZAANGOR SHAMAN
295

| | 3-10 | 2 | 3 | 3/6 |
| | 1 | 4 | 4 | 2/4 |

10 · 4 · 30

CURSELING, EYE OF TZEENTCH
260

| | 3-10 | 2 | 3 | 3/6 |
| | 1 | 4 | 4 | 2/5 |

4 · 5 · 28

OGROID THAUMATURGE
265

| | 3-10 | 2 | 3 | 3/6 |
| | 1 | 4 | 5 | 2/5 |

4 · 4 · 32

FATEMASTER

🗡️	🌀 2	✳️ 4	✊ 4	🛡️ 2/5

250

↗️ 10 · ☀️ 4 · 💀 25

ENLIGHTENED AVIARCH ON FOOT

🏹	🌀 2	✳️ 5	✊ 4	🛡️ 2/4

220

↗️ 5 · ☀️ 4 · 💀 30

KAIRIC ADEPT

🔱 3-10	🌀 3	✳️ 3	✊ 3	🛡️ 1/3
🗡️ 2	🌀 2	✳️ 2	✊ 3	🛡️ 1/4

150

↗️ 4 · ☀️ 4 · 💀 20

ENLIGHTENED AVIARCH ON DISC OF TZEENTCH

🏹	🌀 2	✳️ 5	✊ 4	🛡️ 2/4

260

↗️ 10 · ☀️ 4 · 💀 30

TWISTBRAY

🗡️	🌀 1	✳️ 3	✊ 4	🛡️ 2/4

175

↗️ 5 · ☀️ 4 · 💀 25

SKYFIRE AVIARCH

🏹 3-20	🌀 3	✳️ 4	✊ 4	🛡️ 2/5
🦷	🌀 1	✳️ 4	✊ 4	🛡️ 2/4

280

↗️ 10 · ☀️ 4 · 💀 30

36

TZAANGOR WITH PAIR OF SAVAGE BLADES — 75

⚔	🏹	✶	✊	🛡
1	3	3	1/4

➴ 5 | ☀ 3 | 💀 15

KAIRIC ACOLYTE WITH PAIRED CURSED BLADES — 85

⚡	🏹	✶	✊	🛡
3-10	2	3	1/3
⚔	🏹	✶	✊	🛡
1	4	3	1/3

➴ 4 | ☀ 3 | 💀 10

TZAANGOR WITH SAVAGE BLADE AND ARCANITE SHIELD — 85

⚔	🏹	✶	✊	🛡
1	2	3	1/4

➴ 5 | ☀ 4 | 💀 15

KAIRIC ACOLYTE WITH SCROLL OF DARK ARTS — 135

⚡	🏹	✶	✊	🛡
3-10	4	4	2/4
⚔	🏹	✶	✊	🛡
1	2	3	1/3

➴ 4 | ☀ 4 | 💀 10

TZAANGOR WITH SAVAGE GREATBLADE — 105

⚔	🏹	✶	✊	🛡
1	3	4	2/5

➴ 5 | ☀ 3 | 💀 15

KAIRIC ACOLYTE WITH VULCHARC — 70

⚡	🏹	✶	✊	🛡	
3-10	2	3	1/3	
⚔	🏹	✶	✊	🛡	
1	3	3	1/3	

➴ 4 | ☀ 3 | 💀 10

TZAANGOR MUTANT — 90

⚔	🏹	✶	✊	🛡	
1	4	3	1/4	

➴ 5 | ☀ 3 | 💀 15

TZAANGOR ENLIGHTENED ON FOOT — 150

⚔	🏹	✶	✊	🛡	
2	4	4	2/4	

➴ 5 | ☀ 4 | 💀 20

KAIRIC ACOLYTE WITH CURSED BLADE AND ARCANITE SHIELD — 85

⚡	🏹	✶	✊	🛡
3-10	2	3	1/3
⚔	🏹	✶	✊	🛡
1	3	3	1/3

➴ 4 | ☀ 4 | 💀 10

TZAANGOR ENLIGHTENED ON DISC OF TZEENTCH — 200

⚔	🏹	✶	✊	🛡	
2	4	4	2/4	

➴ 10 | ☀ 4 | 💀 20

KAIRIC ACOLYTE WITH CURSED GLAIVE AND ARCANITE SHIELD — 90

⚡	🏹	✶	✊	🛡
3-10	2	3	1/3
⚔	🏹	✶	✊	🛡
2	2	3	1/4

➴ 4 | ☀ 4 | 💀 10

TZAANGOR SKYFIRE — 235

⚡	🏹	✶	✊	🛡	
3-20	2	4	2/5	
⚔	🏹	✶	✊	🛡	
1	4	4	2/4	

➴ 10 | ☀ 4 | 💀 20

DAEMONS OF TZEENTCH

Gibbering maniacally and hurling bolts of shimmering witchfire, the daemons of Tzeentch are agents of madness and anarchy. These bounding, transient creatures are an assault on all that is rational and sane, crafted from the very essence of magic and manipulation.

DAEMONS OF TZEENTCH FIGHTER ABILITIES

[Double] Locus of Sorcery: Add half the value of this ability (rounding up) to the Strength characteristic of the next attack action made by this fighter this activation that targets an enemy fighter more than 3" away.

[Double] Split: A fighter can use this ability only if they have 1 or more damage points allocated to them. Set up 2 new fighters with the **Disciples of Tzeentch: Daemons** runemark (🔥) and the **Warrior** runemark (✧) on the battlefield within 3" of this fighter. Then, this fighter is taken down. In a campaign battle, do not make an injury roll for this fighter.

[Double] Split Again: A fighter can use this ability only if they have 1 or more damage points allocated to them. Set up 1 new fighter with the **Disciples of Tzeentch: Daemons** runemark (🔥) and the **Minion** runemark (✧) on the battlefield within 3" of this fighter. Then, this fighter is taken down. In a campaign battle, do not make an injury roll for this fighter.

[Triple] Latching Bite: Add the value of this ability to the Strength characteristic of the next attack action made by this fighter this activation. In addition, the target fighter cannot make move or disengage actions until the end of the battle round.

[Quad] Capricious Warpflame: Allocate a number of damage points equal to the value of this ability to all visible enemy fighters within 3" of this fighter.

DAEMONS OF TZEENTCH LEADER ABILITIES

[Double] Blue Fire: Pick a visible enemy fighter within 9" of this fighter and roll 2 dice. For each 4-5, allocate 1 damage point to that fighter. For each 6, allocate a number of damage points to that fighter equal to the value of this ability.

[Triple] Master of Destiny: Until the end of the battle round, add the value of this ability to the value of other abilities (to a maximum of 6) used by friendly fighters within 12" of this fighter.

[Triple] Pink Fire: Pick a visible enemy fighter within 9" of this fighter and roll 9 dice. For each 3+, allocate 1 damage point to that fighter.

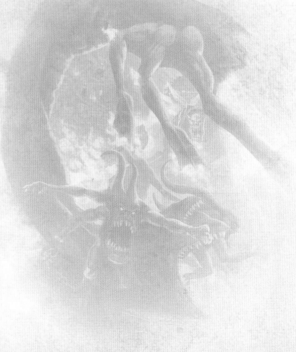

DAEMONS OF TZEENTCH FATETWISTER BANDS

FLUXMASTER
250

🔥 3-10	🌀 2	⚔️ 3	✊ 3/6
〰️	🌀 1	⚔️ 3	✊ 2/4

➶ 12 · ☀️ 3 · 💀 25

CHANGECASTER
180

🔥 3-10	🌀 2	⚔️ 3	✊ 3/6
〰️	🌀 1	⚔️ 3	✊ 2/4

➶ 4 · ☀️ 3 · 💀 22

IRIDESCENT HORROR
190

🔥 3-10	🌀 2	⚔️ 3	✊ 1/4
〰️	🌀 1	⚔️ 4	✊ 2/4

➶ 4 · ☀️ 4 · 💀 22

PYROCASTER
220

🔥 3-10	🌀 4	⚔️ 3	✊ 2/4
🦷	🌀 1	⚔️ 2	✊ 2/4

➶ 8 · ☀️ 3 · 💀 25

SCREAMER OF TZEENTCH
180

〰️ 1	🌀 4	⚔️ 4	✊ 2/4

➶ 12 · ☀️ 3 · 💀 18

PINK HORROR
90

🔥 3-10	🌀 2	⚔️ 3	✊ 1/4
〰️	🌀 1	⚔️ 3	✊ 1/4

➶ 4 · ☀️ 3 · 💀 12

BLUE HORROR
75

🔥 3-10	🌀 2	⚔️ 3	✊ 1/3
〰️	🌀 1	⚔️ 3	✊ 1/3

➶ 4 · ☀️ 3 · 💀 8

BRIMSTONE HORRORS
55

🔥 3-10	🌀 2	⚔️ 3	✊ 1/2
〰️	🌀 1	⚔️ 3	✊ 1/2

➶ 4 · ☀️ 3 · 💀 6

FLAMER OF TZEENTCH
150

🔥 3-10	🌀 3	⚔️ 3	✊ 2/4
🦷	🌀 1	⚔️ 2	✊ 2/4

➶ 8 · ☀️ 3 · 💀 15

EXALTED FLAMER OF TZEENTCH
210

🔥 3-10	🌀 4	⚔️ 3	✊ 2/5
🦷	🌀 1	⚔️ 2	✊ 2/4

➶ 8 · ☀️ 3 · 💀 30

MAGGOTKIN OF NURGLE

Nurgle is the Lord of Despair, the pustulent god of entropy and rot. Wherever the mortal and daemonic children of the Plague Lord walk, sickness and death are sure to follow.

It is difficult, at first, to understand why mortals would willingly offer worship to the Chaos power known as Nurgle. The rotten wood-carvings and festering cave-paintings that portray this foul deity often depict a hideous mountain of blubber and pus, sagging flesh hanging in long, dripping ropes as maggot-infested intestines spill forth from a ruptured stomach. Filth and decay follow in Nurgle's wake, and those who draw the ire of this rancid god are struck down by wasting sickness and the most terrible of maladies.

Yet despite this terrible appearance, Nurgle is revered as a loving father-god by communities of outcasts, the diseased and the destitute across the realms. 'Grandfather' Nurgle, as the Plague Lord is often affectionately known by his followers, is empowered whenever mortals succumb to hopelessness and despair. Nurgle's creed is one of bleak acceptance and comfortable numbness, of wallowing in misery rather than striving to better one's circumstances. In the Mortal Realms, where the spirits of so many cultures were brutally crushed during the horrific trials of the Age of Chaos, the worship of Nurgle finds fertile ground indeed.

Nurgle is obsessed with the cycle of life and death, albeit perverted into ruinous form. The 'gifts' bestowed upon the Grandfather's faithful are poxes, blights and agues of all kinds, manifestations of rampant sickness and entropy that drive the afflicted to hopelessness – and, in turn, into the accepting clutches of the Plague Lord. Flies, maggots and wretched carrion birds are all considered to be Nurgle's creatures, for these are common vectors by which disease is transmitted across the Mortal Realms. In the shadows and sewers of the free cities, cults dedicated to decay work to brew terrible maladies to drain into waterways or transmit through the air via great, smog-belching censers.

Of course, not all of Nurgle's plagues are physical in nature. Soul-poxes and metaphysical blights are all capable of being summoned by the god's most devoted servants. Through these methods they are even capable of infecting the kingdoms of the dead, much to the displeasure of Nagash – and there are some champions of Nurgle who possess true visions of corrupted grandeur, for their goal is nothing less than to infect the very realms themselves through concocting the most potent of all diseases.

All manner of vile creatures pledge allegiance to Nurgle, from outcast beastmen to colonies of abandoned lepers and pox-ridden, but it is the Rotbringer Contagiums who form the finest and most beloved mortal armies of the Plague Lord. These warriors – bloated with foulness and dripping with disease – revel in their Grandfather's favour, typically exhibiting a bleak gallows mirth as they desecrate the land and hew through their fragile foes. Putrid Blightkings form the footsoldiers of the Rotbringers; though they are few in number, each of these rancid warriors has been so blessed by Nurgle that they are the equal to seven lesser men, capable of shrugging off all but the most terrible blows as they swing their befouled weapons. Some Blightkings rise higher in Nurgle's favour still, taking on the mantle of a mighty champion or soaring to battle upon the back of a terrifying, unnatural beast known as a Rot Fly.

Fouler still are Nurgle's daemonic children, for each is a shard of the Plague Lord's own rotten majesty bestowed with sentience. These beings are disease made manifest, and exemplify Nurgle's perverse cycle. Plaguebearers are moribund tallymen compelled to obsessively catalogue each disease and pox they observe. In comparison to their constant droning misery,

the daemonic mites known as Nurglings are possessed of constant unshakeable enthusiasm, swarming across the battlefield to drag down enemies with sharpened fangs and filthy claws. Perhaps the strangest plague daemons are the Beasts of Nurgle – slobbering slug-like creatures whose affections inevitably prove fatal to their hapless mortal 'playmates'.

Of all the Chaos Gods, it is perhaps Nurgle who has the greatest interest in conquering the Eightpoints; the island-between-realms is a continent-sized laboratory for the incubation of new diseases, while the arcways themselves are fine vectors through which to transmit these gifts across the Mortal Realms entire. Still, the Lord of Despair's champions are not given to over-abundant optimism, and few are fool enough to openly challenge Archaon's dominion of the land. Like a poison crawling through a bloodstream, their corrupting efforts are slow, steady, yet no less dangerous for that. Gallowbands of Rotbringers and Befouled Bands of

daemons often focus their efforts upon desecrating shrines and infecting those enemy warriors who encounter them; through these acts of sacrilege, their contagions are transmitted far quicker than the Nurglites could ever manage through simple slaughter.

'Look at it, my children, just look at it! Such hideous cleanliness! Such noxious purity! No, no, no – in Grandfather's name, this will never do!'

- Grombulox the Generous, prior to the befouling of the Ith'amyir Glade

Large areas of Carngrad are little more than disease-ridden slums, and here the followers of Nurgle thrive. More and more inhabitants of that cursed city are brought into the Grandfather's sickly embrace with each turning of the crimson moons. It is said that these degenerates are ruled over by a being known as the Weeping Proctor, though none of the agents sent into the most blighted areas of the city by the Talons of Carngrad have been able to garner more than rumours regarding this enigmatic figure. Indeed, many of them do not return at all…

NURGLE ROTBRINGERS

Only the foulest warriors can hope to gain the pestilent favour of Nurgle. Their bodies are swollen and distended by ravaging plagues, their weapons covered in filth. They advance into battle at a slow but unstoppable pace, chortling in delight as they spread their Grandfather's gifts.

NURGLE ROTBRINGERS FIGHTER ABILITIES	
	[Double] Virulent Discharge: Pick a visible enemy fighter within 1" of this fighter and roll a number of dice equal to the value of this ability. For each 4+, allocate 1 damage point to that fighter.
	[Double] Venomous Sting: Pick a visible enemy fighter within 1" of this fighter and roll a dice. On a 2+, until the end of this battle round, that fighter cannot make move actions or disengage actions.
	[Double] Toll the Sonorous Tocsin: Until the end of the battle round, add 1 to the Move characteristic of move actions made by friendly fighters that start within 6" of this fighter.
	[Triple] Blighted Icon: Until the end of the battle round, add 1 to the Toughness characteristic of friendly fighters while they are within 6" of this fighter.
	[Quad] Unnatural Regeneration: A fighter cannot use this ability if they are within 1" of any enemy fighters. Remove a number of damage points allocated to this fighter equal to double the value of this ability.

NURGLE ROTBRINGERS LEADER ABILITIES	
	[Double] Thrice-ripened Death's Head: Pick a visible enemy fighter within 6" of this fighter and roll 2 dice. For each 4-5, allocate 1 damage point to that fighter. For each 6, allocate a number of damage points to that fighter equal to the value of this ability.
	[Double] Stream of Corruption: Pick a visible enemy fighter within 9" of this fighter and roll a number of dice equal to the value of this ability. For each 5+, allocate 1 damage point to that fighter and, until the end of the battle round, subtract 1 from that fighter's Toughness characteristic (to a minimum of 1).
	[Triple] Grandfather's Blessing: Until the end of the battle round, add 1 to the Strength characteristic of attack actions that have a Range characteristic of 3 or less made by friendly fighters while they are within 6" of this fighter.
	[Triple] Rotsword Stab: This fighter can make a bonus attack action that has a Range characteristic of 3 or less. If that bonus attack action scores any critical hits, roll a dice. On a 4+, subtract 1 from the Move characteristic (to a minimum of 1) of the target fighter for the rest of the battle.

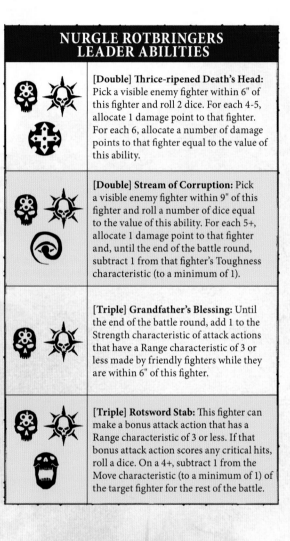

NURGLE ROTBRINGERS GALLOWBANDS

LORD OF PLAGUES
205

⚔	↻	✳	✊	⚔
1	3	5	3/5
↗ 3 ☀ 4 💀 32

PUTRID BLIGHTKING WITH BLIGHTED WEAPON
135

⚔	↻	✳	✊	⚔
1	3	4	2/4
↗ 3 ☀ 4 💀 25

LORD OF BLIGHTS
210

⚒	↻	✳	✊	⚔
1	3	4	2/5
↗ 3 ☀ 5 💀 32

PUTRID BLIGHTKING WITH FILTH-ENCRUSTED SHIELD
145

⚔	↻	✳	✊	⚔
1	2	4	2/4
↗ 3 ☀ 5 💀 25

LORD OF AFFLICTIONS
290

⚔	↻	✳	✊	⚔
2	4	4	3/5
↗ 6 ☀ 4 💀 42

PUTRID BLIGHTKING WITH SONOROUS TOCSIN
145
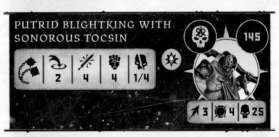
●	↻	✳	✊	⚔
2	4	4	1/4
↗ 3 ☀ 4 💀 25

ROTBRINGER SORCERER
165

⚡	↻	✳	✊	⚔
3-7	2	3	3/6
🔨	↻	✳	✊	⚔
2	3	3	1/4
↗ 3 ☀ 3 💀 22

PUTRID BLIGHTKING ICON BEARER
140

🗡	↻	✳	✊	⚔
1	3	4	2/4
↗ 3 ☀ 4 💀 25

HARBINGER OF DECAY
195

🗡	↻	✳	✊	⚔
2	3	4	2/4
↗ 6 ☀ 4 💀 25

PUSGOYLE BLIGHTLORD
245

🗡	↻	✳	✊	⚔
2	4	4	2/5
↗ 6 ☀ 4 💀 40

PUTRID BLIGHTKING BLIGHTLORD
190

⚔	↻	✳	✊	⚔
1	4	4	2/5
↗ 3 ☀ 4 💀 30

DAEMONS OF NURGLE

The daemons of Nurgle trudge, caper and slither to battle amidst the sound of gloomy droning, buzzing flies and clanging bells. All of them are frightening propositions in battle, for they are nearly impossible to slay and even the merest scratch from their pestilent weapons can prove fatal.

DAEMONS OF NURGLE FIGHTER ABILITIES	
	[Double] Disgustingly Resilient: Roll a number of dice equal to the value of this ability. For each 4+, remove 1 damage point allocated to this fighter.
	[Double] Acidic Slime Trail: Pick a visible enemy fighter within 1" of this fighter. This fighter makes a bonus disengage action. Then, allocate a number of damage points to that fighter equal to the value of this ability.
	[Double] Venomous Sting: Pick a visible enemy fighter within 1" of this fighter and roll a dice. On a 2+, until the end of this battle round, that fighter cannot make move actions or disengage actions.
	[Triple] Cloud of Flies: Until the end of the battle round, subtract 1 from the Attacks characteristic (to a minimum of 1) of attack actions that target this fighter.
	[Quad] Endless Swarm: Remove a number of damage points allocated to this fighter equal to double the value of this ability.

DAEMONS OF NURGLE LEADER ABILITIES	
	[Double] Jolly Gutpipes: Until the end of the battle round, add 1 to the Move characteristic of move actions made by friendly fighters that start within 6" of this fighter.
	[Triple] Grandfather's Blessing: Until the end of the battle round, add 1 to the Strength characteristic of attack actions that have a Range characteristic of 3 or less made by friendly fighters while they are within 6" of this fighter.
	[Triple] Menacing Overseer: Until the end of the battle round, add 1 to the Attacks characteristic of attack actions that have a Range characteristic of 3 or less made by friendly fighters while they are within 9" of this fighter.
	[Quad] Disgusting Sneeze: Pick a visible enemy fighter within 9" of this fighter and roll a number of dice equal to the value of this ability. For each 2+, allocate 2 damage points to that fighter.

DAEMONS OF NURGLE BEFOULED BANDS

POXBRINGER — 195

3-7	2	3	3/6
1	1	4	2/5

3 | 4 | 22

BEAST OF NURGLE — 175

1	4	4	2/4

4 | 4 | 30

SPOILPOX SCRIVENER — 175

1	2	5	3/5

3 | 4 | 22

PLAGUE DRONE — 170

1	3	3	1/4

6 | 4 | 30

SLOPPITY BILEPIPER — 165

1	3	4	2/4

4 | 4 | 22

NURGLINGS — 145

1	6	3	1/3

5 | 3 | 30

PLAGUERIDDEN — 120

1	4	3	2/4

3 | 3 | 20

PLAGUEBRINGER — 230

1	4	3	2/4

6 | 4 | 35

PLAGUEBEARER — 50

1	3	3	1/4

3 | 3 | 10

HEDONITES OF SLAANESH

The Hedonites of Slaanesh are epicureans and revellers of the foulest kind. Their warbands are populated by cruel daemons and frenzied mortals, and they delight in spreading depravity wherever they tread.

Of all the Dark Gods, Slaanesh is perhaps the most insidious. The sphere of this atavistic entity is no single emotional concept, as is the case with the other Ruinous Powers, but instead all the various aspects of the mortal psyche taken to the most extreme degree. Rage, mania, lust, agony – all of these sensations and more beside serve to empower this hungering deity when they are experienced with sufficient fervour.

Known to many as the Dark Prince, Slaanesh is beguiling as only an immortal can be. Slender-limbed and androgynous, the worship of Slaanesh initially asks only that supplicants pursue their innermost desires without restraint or regret. It is easy to understand, therefore, why Slaanesh's worship is so prominent amongst so-called bastions of civilisation. Failing

artists, struggling playwrights and overworked citizens all look to Slaanesh to provide a muse or simple succour; the pleasures they experience in these clandestine, cultic gatherings can at first seem benign enough, a blessed reprieve from the toil of everyday existence.

Yet such dabbling is the first step on a terminal path, for these devotees will soon come to learn of Slaanesh's terrible hunger. The further a mortal descends into the Dark Prince's worship, the more they find themselves unable to take satisfaction in anything but the most extreme acts. Beauteous maidens willingly disfigure themselves as they chase indefinable standards of perfection, while gourmets are driven to seek new and forbidden tastes. Gradually, the lure of new and excessive experiences comes to claim

these supplicants utterly, driving them deeper into ecstatic madness until even the greatest of atrocities seems trite and mundane.

In ancient days, the Dark Prince stood proud amongst the pantheon of Chaos. However, as the Age of Sigmar rages, Slaanesh's throne sits empty. Towards the waning years of the Age of Myth, the aelven pantheon – whose people had been devoured by the Chaos God during the destruction of the world-that-was – devised a cunning scheme to imprison Slaanesh in a crepuscular prison between the realms of Light and Shadow. Binding the god with six-hundred-and-sixty-six mystic chains of entwined Hyshian and Ulguan magic, the aelven powers began the slow process of extracting the devoured souls of their people from Slaanesh's divine form.

This has continued for many long centuries, but the Dark Prince has not simply languished in incarceration. Secretly, Slaanesh has begun shattering these chains through the engineering of seemingly impossible events, in doing so sundering the paradoxical magic that forms the fetters. Should enough of them be broken, the god will be able to escape through sheer might. The consequences of this for all the inhabitants of the realms would be dire indeed.

In the Dark Prince's absence, hosts of Hedonites gather to spread their depraved creed. Their armies can roughly be divided into three categories, dictated by their ultimate goals and the personalities of those daemonic and mortal champions that lead them. The Invaders care little for the fate of lost Slaanesh, or indeed anything aside from revelling in the myriad sensations provided by battle and conquest. Pretender hosts are ruled by the mightiest of Slaanesh's champions,

each convinced that they alone are the true heir to their master's empty throne. Godseekers, meanwhile, have devoted themselves to tracking down their absent deity, though many are soon distracted by the thrill of the chase. Across the realms they follow all manner of supposed clues and scent-trails – though none have yet breached Slaanesh's prison, their blistering speed means they are often the first to sample all manner of new vices and sensations.

Most Slaaneshi warbands are comprised of mortal devotees known as Sybarites. From the lowliest Blissbarb Archer to the mightiest champion, they exemplify their own fascinations to a horrific extent on the field of battle – from the supremely swift Slickblade Seekers to the pain-obsessed blademasters of the Myrmidesh and their egotistical, daemon-touched Symbaresh kin. Should the Sybarites spread sufficient pain and vile pleasure, the darkling daemons of the Dark Prince may be drawn from their silken pavilions of torment. The most common of these are the Daemonettes. Known as the handmaidens of the Dark Prince, these androgynous beings possess a hypnotic allure that, coupled with their otherworldly grace and chitinous claws, allows them to slice apart a host of foes before a weapon can even be raised against them. Some Daemonettes take to battle atop swift steeds of Slaanesh; these soul-hunting Seekers ride alongside trilling, chimerical monsters known as Fiends. Fashioned from lurid nightmares, Fiends possess a range of unnatural weapons with which to slaughter their prey, not least of

which is the soporific musk they secrete, which lures mortals into a dream-like fugue.

The Hedonite hosts are typically drawn to the most extreme of environments, and so it is little surprise that they have established a strong presence throughout the Bloodwind Spoil. Whether they be bands of Sybarites, known as Dark Revellers, searching for fresh experiences and fetching realmstone trinkets, or daemons seeking new souls to feast upon, no opportunity to exercise excessive cruelty is ever passed up. They revel in any chance to prove their superiority, particularly over those pledged to the worship of Khorne, for the Blood God and Slaanesh share a mutual animosity that frequently manifests as violence. Aelves too are favoured prey, and many Hedonite warbands seek out ancient Khainite temples hidden beneath the tortured earth, for they know that the blood-cultists often launch expeditions to such places in search of lost secrets.

'Rejoice in the ruptures and roguish revels resulting from ravishing raptures. Listen to the lurid lays and let lingering lusts lure you to lapses of loyalty. Slay in search of sensation! Sin while seeking sordid satisfaction! Scream! Scream for Slaanesh!'

- Marlion Leguara, the Bleeding Baritone

The mysterious soul-engine found in the western reaches of the Skullpike Mountains, known as the Screaming Coil, has long been held by sensation-worshipping cultists of Slaanesh. This device is nothing less than a divine gift in the eyes of the Hedonites, for it possesses the power to send waves of agony spreading across the Bloodwind Spoil. However, the egotistical nature of Slaanesh's chosen ensures that all believe that they alone know best how to harness the device, and thus many Hedonite warbands battle amongst themselves for control of the Screaming Coil, each seeking to turn it to their own perverse ends.

SLAANESH SYBARITES

Those mortals dedicated to Slaanesh are amongst the most unnerving servants of all the Dark Gods. In their pursuit of the sensation, these scions of torment gleefully commit the most terrible acts imaginable in search of ecstasy. Yet this contentment withers away as swiftly as it comes, and so the Sybarites ply their agonising talents far and wide – laughing maniacally as their foes scream themselves bloody and raw in pain.

SLAANESH SYBARITES FIGHTER ABILITIES

 [Double] Unrivalled Velocity: Add half the value of this ability (rounding up) to the Move characteristic of this fighter for the next move action they make this activation.

 [Triple] Dance of the Wailing Blade: Add 1 to the damage points allocated by each hit and critical hit from attack actions made by this fighter this activation that have a Range characteristic of 3 or less.

 [Triple] Slaves to Impulse: A fighter can use this ability only if there is a visible enemy fighter within 6" of them. This fighter makes a bonus move action and must finish closer to the closest visible enemy fighter than they were at the start of that move action.

 [Triple] Impaling Strike: Until the end of this fighter's activation, the next time this fighter finishes a move action within 1" of an enemy fighter, pick a visible enemy fighter within 1" of this fighter. Allocate a number of damage points to that fighter equal to the value of this ability.

 [Triple] Volley of Tearing Blades: Add half the value of this ability (rounding up) to the Attacks characteristic of the next attack action made by this fighter this activation that targets an enemy fighter more than 3" away.

 [Quad] Ego-driven Excess: This fighter can make a bonus move action or a bonus attack action. In addition, each time a fighter is taken down by an attack action made by this fighter this activation, this fighter can make a further bonus move action or bonus attack action.

SLAANESH SYBARITES LEADER ABILITIES

 [Double] Violence and Excess: A fighter can use this ability only if an enemy fighter has been taken down by an attack action made by them this activation. This fighter makes a bonus move action or a bonus attack action.

 [Triple] Tendrils of Unnatural Smoke: Until the end of the battle round, subtract 1 from the Attacks characteristic (to a minimum of 1) of attack actions made by enemy fighters while they are within 6" of this fighter.

 [Triple] Paragon of Depravity: Until the end of the battle round, add the value of this ability to the Strength characteristic of attack actions that have a Range characteristic of 3 or less made by friendly fighters while they are within 6" of this fighter.

SLAANESH SYBARITES DARK REVELLERS

SHARDSPEAKER — 170

3-7	2	3	3/6
2	3	3	1/4

4 · 3 · 22

LORD OF PAIN — 220

2	4	5	3/5

4 · 4 · 25

HELLREAVER WITH CLAW-SPEAR — 235

2	4	4	2/4

10 · 4 · 30

BLISSBARB ARCHER HIGH TEMPTER — 130

3-15	3	3	1/4
1	3	3	1/3

5 · 3 · 16

SLAANGOR SLAKE-HORN — 225

1	4	4	3/5

6 · 4 · 30

SLICKBLADE HUNTER-SEEKER — 240

2	4	3	2/4

10 · 4 · 35

BLISSBARB SEEKER HIGH TEMPTER — 220

3-15	3	3	1/4
1	3	3	1/3

10 · 3 · 35

MYRMIDESH PAINMASTER — 205

1	4	4	2/4

4 · 5 · 25

SYMBARESH EGOPOMP — 200

2	4	5	2/4

4 · 4 · 25

HELLSTRIDER WITH CLAW-SPEAR

	2	3	3	1/4

145

10 | 4 | 20

HELLSTRIDER WITH HELLSCOURGE

	3	4	3	1/3

145

10 | 4 | 20

BLISSBARB ARCHER

3-15	2	3	1/3	
1	3	3	1/3	

80

5 | 3 | 8

SLAANGOR FIENDBLOOD

	1	4	4	2/5

165

6 | 4 | 20

SLICKBLADE SEEKER

	2	3	3	2/4

180

10 | 4 | 20

BLISSBARB SEEKER

3-15	2	3	1/3	
1	3	3	1/3	

165

10 | 3 | 25

MYRMIDESH PAINBRINGER

140

🪓	🗡️	✴️	👊	🛡️
	1	4	3	2/4

➤ 4 | ☀️ 5 | 💀 15

SYMBARESH TWINSOUL WITH EXCRUCIATOR LASH

115

⛓️	🗡️	✴️	👊	🛡️
	3	4	3	1/4

➤ 4 | ☀️ 4 | 💀 15

SYMBARESH TWINSOUL WITH MERCILESS BLADES

130

🗡️	🗡️	✴️	👊	🛡️
	1	4	4	2/4

➤ 4 | ☀️ 4 | 💀 15

SYMBARESH TWINSOUL WITH SINFUL CLEAVER

130

🗡️	🗡️	✴️	👊	🛡️
	1	3	5	2/4

➤ 4 | ☀️ 4 | 💀 15

DAEMONS OF SLAANESH

Quicksilver fast, the Daemons of Slaanesh are driven to a manic state of ecstasy by the myriad sensations only battle can provide. Each is a shard of the Dark Prince devoted to spreading his creed throughout the realms. The feeling of flesh parting under the caress of their razor-sharp claws is a rapturous wonder to these creatures, and where they tread the battlefield is filled with wicked laughter, the daemons energised by the arterial spray of hot blood across their sinuous forms.

DAEMONS OF SLAANESH FIGHTER ABILITIES

[Double] Lithe and Swift: Add half the value of this ability (rounding up) to the Move characteristic of this fighter for the next move action they make this activation.

[Double] Sadistic Killers: Add 1 to the damage points allocated by each hit and critical hit from attack actions made by this fighter this activation that have a Range characteristic of 3 or less.

[Double] Crushing Grip: Pick a visible enemy fighter within 1" of this fighter and roll a dice. On a 2+, until the end of the battle round, that fighter cannot make move actions or disengage actions.

[Triple] Impaling Strike: Until the end of this fighter's activation, the next time this fighter finishes a move action within 1" of an enemy fighter, pick a visible enemy fighter within 1" of this fighter. Allocate a number of damage points to that fighter equal to the value of this ability.

[Quad] Deadly Venom: Until the end of this fighter's activation, add half the value of this ability (rounding up) to the damage points allocated by critical hits from attack actions made by this fighter. In addition, after each attack action made by this fighter, roll a dice. On a 5+, until the end of this battle round, the target fighter cannot make move actions or disengage actions.

DAEMONS OF SLAANESH LEADER ABILITIES

[Double] Discordant Disruption: Until the end of the battle round, subtract 1 from the Attacks characteristic (to a minimum of 1) of attack actions made by enemy fighters while they are within 6" of this fighter.

[Triple] Locus of Excruciation: Until the end of the battle round, add 1 to the Strength characteristic of attack actions that have a Range characteristic of 3 or less made by friendly fighters while they are within 6" of this fighter.

[Triple] Mirror of Absorption: Pick a visible enemy fighter that has not activated this battle round that is within 9" of this fighter. That fighter is said to have activated.

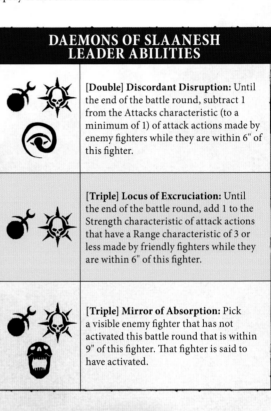

THE CONTORTED EPITOME — 250

| | 3-7 | 2 | 3 | 3/6 |
| | 1 | 6 | 3 | 2/4 |

10 | 3 | 28

DAEMONETTE — 75

| | 1 | 4 | 3 | 1/4 |

5 | 3 | 10

INFERNAL ENRAPTURESS — 170

| | 3-12 | 4 | 3 | 1/4 |
| | 1 | 3 | 3 | 2/4 |

4 | 3 | 22

FIEND — 150

| | 1 | 4 | 3 | 1/4 |

8 | 3 | 30

VICELEADER — 190

| | 3-7 | 2 | 3 | 3/6 |
| | 1 | 5 | 3 | 2/4 |

5 | 3 | 22

SEEKER OF SLAANESH — 130

| | 1 | 4 | 3 | 1/4 |

10 | 3 | 20

ALLURER — 145

| | 1 | 5 | 3 | 2/4 |

5 | 3 | 20

HELLREAVER WITH CLAW-SPEAR — 235

| | 2 | 4 | 4 | 2/4 |

10 | 4 | 30

BLISSBRINGER — 220

| | 1 | 5 | 3 | 2/4 |

8 | 3 | 35

HELLSTRIDER WITH CLAW-SPEAR — 145

| | 2 | 3 | 3 | 1/4 |

10 | 4 | 20

HEARTSEEKER — 205

| | 1 | 5 | 3 | 2/4 |

10 | 3 | 30

HELLSTRIDER WITH HELLSCOURGE — 145

| | 3 | 4 | 3 | 1/3 |

10 | 4 | 20

SKAVEN

The skaven gnaw at the roots of reality, forever plotting and scheming to achieve greater power. Armed with sinister cunning, vast numbers and diabolical weapons of war, these ratmen are a plague on civilisation.

In the taphouses of Sigmar's cities, veteran Freeguilders and sewer wardens speak in hushed tones of rats that walk as men. Most civilised folk dismiss these stories as deranged fantasy or, at worst, some verminous breed of beastmen, but the truth is far more dire. From the sub-realm of Blight City, the skaven have steadily expanded their influence across the Mortal Realms. Their beady red eyes watch from the shadows, agile minds forever working to overthrow civilisation and install their own malevolent regime in its place. Such is the will of the Great Horned Rat, the treacherous god of the skaven and newest member of the Chaos pantheon, who desires nothing more than to spread wasting ruin to every corner of reality.

Every skaven firmly believes in two essential truths; that they are the greatest being that has ever lived, and that everything else – be it living or dead – is a rival who wishes to overthrow them. This paranoia is justified, of course, by the fact that all skaven – from the lowliest slave to the mightiest Lord of Decay – really are constantly conspiring to overthrow their fellows and claim power for themselves. They are devious, spiteful creatures devoid of anything resembling honour, each utterly concerned with their own supremacy – and willing to do anything to ensure it, no matter how vile. It takes a powerful leader to unite even a small warband, or Scurrypack, of skaven in pursuit of a single goal, and they will only remain in control so long as they can effectively demonstrate their might and deal with any challengers. Those skaven rulers who make a mistake rarely have the chance to do so twice.

Skaven society is clan-based, with each grouping typically mirroring or owing fealty to one of the original Greater Clans. The Clans Verminus provide the seemingly endless numbers of skavendom. Vicious Clawlords lead hordes of Clanrats and elite Stormvermin into battle; skaven are by nature cowardly, and primarily concerned with protecting their own hides. When they gather in great numbers, however, they are overcome with a form of rabid bravery that sees them overwhelm their foes in a seething mass.

The vast armies of the Clans Verminus are bolstered by the more specialised elements of skaven society. The Clans Moulder are flesh-crafters and masters of mutation. From their subterranean laboratories emerge packs of hideous bioengineered warbeasts, each brought to life through the use of warpstone – the corrupting realmstone of Blight City. The Clans Skryre also covet warpstone, but seek to turn it to very different ends. These are the dark engineers and technoarcane innovators of the ratmen. They are responsible

for developing much of the strange technology that allows Blight City to function, from portable communication devices known as farsqueakers to entire underground transportation networks. The Clans Skryre, however, are most known – and most feared – for their impressive arsenal of wonder-weapons. From flame-belching Warpfire Throwers to long jezzail rifles and the bizarre rolling creations known as Doomwheels, the volatile death machines of the Skryre clans are often as deadly to the wielder as they are to the target – but life is cheap in skaven society, and the destructive power of these contraptions is often considered well worth the risk.

'Aye, they're down there. Lurking beneath the streets or just out of sight. You might not see them, but mark my words lad, they see you. Watching, always watching, scuttling about in the darkness beneath our homes and our high walls. The forge council might claim that it's the walking woods or the rotlings we should worry about, but don't be fooled. If the ratmen aren't flushed out soon, they'll murder us all in our beds.'

– Jorun Blest, sewer warden of Greywater Fastness

The Clans Pestilens are zealous devotees of all things rancid. They have typically been amongst the greatest and most troublesome powers in skavendom, for their fanatical faith in the Great Corruptor – as they know the Horned Rat – makes them mighty indeed. Their chanting priests lead foul congregations in search of the Thirteen Great Plagues; should all these ancient maladies be assembled, the realms will perish in a cascade of withering decay. Perhaps the most feared of the Greater Clans, however, are the mysterious Clans Eshin. Little is known of these black-clad ratmen, save that they serve the Masterclan – a cabal of cunning prophets and sorcerers known as Grey Seers, whose diabolical schemes have doomed entire empires

– as assassins and spymasters. Yet the Eshin clans are no one's puppets, and it is impossible to know their true agenda – especially since anyone, skaven or otherwise, who digs too deeply into their secrets inevitably turns up with their throat slit.

One of the skaven's greatest centres of power in the Eightpoints can be found in Carngrad – or, more accurately, beneath it. Under the ramshackle streets of the city runs a labyrinthine warren of tunnels and nests, in which numerous skaven clans lurk and battle for supremacy. Known as Under-Carngrad or the Screaming Delve, the Clawlords and Grey Seers who rule these tunnels have negotiated many claw-pacts and treaties with the Talons of Carngrad, maintaining a precarious balance of power punctuated by vicious back-alley confrontation between rival gangs of killers. Being skaven, the lords of the Screaming Delve cannot help but plan to overthrow the Talons and claim the entire city as their own. Perhaps the only thing preventing this is their own fractious nature, for each clan naturally wishes to lead – from the back, of course – when the uprising comes.

The Clans Moulder in particular have an interest in the Eightpoints. Since the discovery of varanite – the mutative molten realmstone native to Archaon's domain – many Master Moulders have coveted the substance as an alternative to warpstone in fuelling their biological experiments. Scurrypacks are assembled by these skaven, or those who wish to curry favour with the Clans Moulder, for the purpose of locating and recovering varanite samples. Some Master Moulders have even hired warriors from outside skavendom for this task. Though such mercenaries are costly, they often prove worth the investment – especially since their employers invariably attempt to have them murdered in the night and take both the realmstone and the payment for themselves.

 SKAVEN

The diabolical schemes of the skaven are a blight on the Mortal Realms. Through the use of deadly contagions, arcane technology, hideous monsters and sheer weight of numbers, these conniving ratmen may achieve their grand plans of ultimate domination yet.

SKAVEN FIGHTER ABILITIES

[Double] Scurry Away: A fighter can use this ability only if they are within 3" of an enemy fighter. Roll a dice. On a 4+, this fighter makes a bonus disengage action.

[Double] Crack the Whip: Pick a visible friendly fighter with the **Beast** runemark (🐀) within 4" of this fighter. That fighter makes a bonus attack action that has a Range characteristic of 3 or less.

[Triple] Crushing Charge: Until the end of this fighter's activation, the next time this fighter finishes a move action within 1" of an enemy fighter, pick a visible enemy fighter within 1" of this fighter. Allocate a number of damage points to that fighter equal to the value of this ability.

[Double] Hired Bodyguard: Until the end of the battle round, friendly fighters with the **Leader** runemark (🔆) cannot be targeted while they are within 1" of this fighter.

[Triple] Poisonous Fumes: Roll a dice for each visible enemy fighter within 3" of this fighter. On a 3+, allocate a number of damage points equal to half the value of this ability (rounding up) to that fighter.

[Quad] Expend Warpstone Spark Canister: This fighter makes a bonus attack action. In addition, add half the value of this ability (rounding up) to the damage points allocated by each hit and critical hit from that attack action.

SKAVEN LEADER ABILITIES

[Double] Consume Warpstone Token: Roll a number of dice equal to the value of this ability. For each roll of 1, allocate 1 damage point to this fighter. For each roll of 4+, add 1 to the damage points allocated to enemy fighters by each hit or critical hit from the next attack action made by this fighter this activation that has a Range characteristic of 3 or more.

[Double] Warp Lightning: Pick a number of visible enemy fighters equal to the value of this ability. The first fighter picked must be within 6" of this fighter, and each subsequent fighter picked must be within 3" of a fighter that has already been picked. The same fighter cannot be picked more than once. Allocate 1 damage point to each fighter picked.

[Double] Flesh-mend: Pick a visible friendly fighter with the **Beast** runemark (🐀) within 4" of this fighter. Remove a number of damage points allocated to that fighter equal to half the value of this ability (rounding up).

[Triple] Running Death: This fighter makes a bonus move action or bonus disengage action. In addition, until the end of this fighter's activation, add 1 to the damage points allocated by critical hits from attack actions made by this fighter.

[Triple] Lead from the Back: Until the end of the battle round, add half the value of this ability (rounding up) to the Attacks characteristic of attack actions that have a Range characteristic of 3 or less made by other friendly fighters while they are within 3" of this fighter.

[Quad] Recite from the Book of Woes: Until the end of the battle round, enemy fighters cannot use abilities while they are within 3" of this fighter.

SKAVEN SCURRYPACKS

GREY SEER — 175

CLAWLORD — 180

ARCH-WARLOCK — 185

CLAWLEADER — 145

WARLOCK ENGINEER — 165

FANGLEADER — 170

WARLOCK BOMBARDIER — 170

MASTER MOULDER — 140

PLAGUE PRIEST — 180

DEATHMASTER — 200

BRINGER OF THE WORD — 150

NIGHTLEADER — 165

STORMFIEND WITH GRINDERFISTS

	1	4	5	4/8

265

5 | 5 | 35

SKRYRE ACOLYTE

3-6	1	4	3/6
1	2	3	1/2

105

6 | 3 | 8

STORMFIEND WITH DOOMFLAYER GAUNTLETS

	1	5	4	4/8

265

5 | 5 | 35

WARPLOCK JEZZAIL

6-20	1	4	4/10
1	2	3	1/2

165

6 | 3 | 12

STORMFIEND WITH SHOCK GAUNTLETS

	1	4	4	4/10

265

5 | 5 | 35

PLAGUE MONK WITH PAIR OF FOETID BLADES

	1	4	3	1/4

70

6 | 3 | 8

STORMFIEND WITH RATLING CANNONS

3-10	4	4	2/4
1	2	4	4/8

285

5 | 5 | 35

PLAGUE MONK WITH FOETID BLADE AND WOE-STAVE

	2	3	3	1/5

70

6 | 3 | 8

STORMFIEND WITH WINDLAUNCHERS

3-20	2	4	2/4
1	2	4	4/8

265

5 | 5 | 35

PLAGUE CENSER BEARER

	2	3	4	2/4

90

6 | 3 | 8

STORMFIEND WITH WARPFIRE PROJECTORS

3-8	2	5	3/6
1	2	4	4/8

265

5 | 5 | 35

CLANRAT WITH RUSTY SPEAR

	2	2	3	1/4

75

6 | 4 | 8

CLANRAT WITH RUSTY BLADE — 75

🗡	🗯	✴	✊	🛡
1	3	3	1/3

↗ 6 · ☀ 4 · 💀 8

GIANT RAT — 35

🦷	🗯	✴	✊	🛡
1	3	3	1/3

↗ 8 · ☀ 2 · 💀 4

STORMVERMIN WITH RUSTY HALBERD — 105

⚔	🗯	✴	✊	🛡
2	3	3	2/4

↗ 6 · ☀ 4 · 💀 10

NIGHT RUNNER — 75

🏹	🗯	✴	✊	🛡
8	2	3	1/2
🗡	🗯	✴	✊	🛡
1	3	3	1/3

↗ 6 · ☀ 3 · 💀 8

STORMVERMIN WITH RUSTY HALBERD AND CLANSHIELD — 115

⚔	🗯	✴	✊	🛡
2	2	3	2/4

↗ 6 · ☀ 5 · 💀 10

GUTTER RUNNER — 95

🏹	🗯	✴	✊	🛡
8	2	3	1/3
🗡	🗯	✴	✊	🛡
1	4	3	1/4

↗ 6 · ☀ 3 · 💀 10

PACKMASTER — 65

⛓	🗯	✴	✊	🛡
3	3	3	1/2
🦷	🗯	✴	✊	🛡
1	3	3	1/3

↗ 6 · ☀ 3 · 💀 8

WARPFIRE THROWER — 105

🔥	✴	✊	🛡
8	3	4	1/4

↗ 6 · ☀ 3 · 💀 12

RAT OGOR — 225

🐾	🗯	✴	✊	🛡
1	4	4	4/8

↗ 5 · ☀ 4 · 💀 30

WARP-GRINDER — 120

🪲	🗯	✴	✊	🛡
1	4	5	2/5

↗ 6 · ☀ 3 · 💀 12

RAT OGOR WITH WARPFIRE GUN — 235

🔥	🗯	✴	✊	🛡
3-8	2	5	3/6
🐾	🗯	✴	✊	🛡
1	2	4	4/8

↗ 5 · ☀ 4 · 💀 30

DOOM-FLAYER — 175

🗡	🗯	✴	✊	🛡
1	5	5	2/4

↗ 7 · ☀ 4 · 💀 18

SLAVES TO DARKNESS

The Slaves to Darkness are conquerors and warlords, infernal champions who walk the Path to Glory. Their cultures have spread far across the Mortal Realms, and they worship the Dark Gods in a variety of ways.

When Sigmar sealed the gates to Azyr, he left the majority of his people to face the predations of Chaos alone. Many of these abandoned souls pledged themselves to the Dark Gods – at first simply to survive, but in time in pursuit of power. Through swearing infernal pacts and committing great acts of carnage, these mortals walk the Path to Glory. Only three possible outcomes wait at the end of this long and terrible road: either the champion will perish, devolve into a hideous beast of roiling flesh known as Chaos Spawn or, in the rarest of cases, become so imbued with the blessings of the gods that they are reborn as an immortal Daemon Prince. So tempting is this final reward that a champion will do and risk anything to achieve it. Better to be the conqueror, after all, than the pitiful conquered.

It would be foolish to believe the Slaves to Darkness to be a monolithic people; amongst their numbers are counted savage barbarian tribes, fallen knightly orders and lore-hungry cabalists, all moulded by the lands they have conquered and by the will of their overlords.

'Come then, stormling! Come and face Karsus the Axe! And when I send you back to your craven thunder god, tell him that I have not forgotten his cowardice!'

- Karsus the Axe, the Butcher of Ahramentia

Greatest of the champions of Chaos is Archaon, and it is he who masterminded the conquest of the Eightpoints in ages past. His armies march endlessly down the great highways that connect the Varanspire with the arcways. It is the goal of many who dwell in the Eightpoints to join Archaon's hosts – these warriors must fight fiercely to prove themselves, for the dark captains of the Everchosen's legions will only accept the best amongst their conquering hordes.

As a champion ascends the Path to Glory, they will receive all manner of gifts from the gods. These can take any form, from suits of rune-marked armour and Chaos-tainted steeds to lashing tentacles, sharp tusks or even stranger 'rewards'. The Chaos Gods are not easily predicted, nor are they restrained in the nature of their gifts; it is difficult to know what will please these dread beings, and many champions have been violently unmade simply through being

overwhelmed by the mutative caress of the Ruinous Powers.

Though the anarchic nature of Chaos means that champions tend to be highly idiosyncratic, there is one thing, however, that unites all those who attain glory under the gaze of the gods – a dark charisma that draws lesser warriors to them from leagues around. It is the nature of power to be attracted to power. Those who seek to step upon the Path to Glory themselves often begin by fighting in the warband – sometimes known as a 'Swordband' – of a greater chieftain or champion. By serving their warleader in their quest for glory they gain the opportunity to excel themselves, and in doing so catch the gaze of the Dark Gods. The Ruinous Powers have little concern for mortal follies such as honour and loyalty; a warrior who rises through the ranks by mounting successful leadership challenges or through cunning treachery is liable to be just as favoured as one who wins their place through more traditional means. So it is that even the most successful champions of Chaos must forever keep one eye on the ranks of their own supporters, for it is from here – particularly the Chosen and subordinate warleaders – that a worthy competitor for the attention of the gods is likely to emerge.

The archetypal image of the Slaves to Darkness amongst the civilised Sigmarite nations is that of barbarous tribes of battle-hungry killers. This is an understandable conceit, for the Marauders who fill out the majority of these tribes have been fighting all their lives to survive in the twisted dominion of Chaos, and when the call to war is sounded it is inevitably they who first hurl themselves against the Cities of Sigmar. Though they are but men, Marauders are savage fighters who seek to honour their tribal pantheon – in reality, the gods of Chaos interpreted through a myriad of cultural lenses – with each fall of their heavy axes. Some amongst their number ride to war on swift stallions drawn from the steppes of the realms, and delight in chasing down any who would flee before the gaze of the dark powers.

Those tribesmen who fully devote themselves to Chaos are an order of magnitude more deadly still. Clad in thick suits of rune-marked armour, these Chaos Warriors and mounted Knights are capable of slaughtering several lesser men with ease, and can even match Sigmar's Stormcasts blade for blade. Many have been marked by their patron deities, and can draw upon a measure of their power. The greatest of their number wield cursed runeblades, ride upon reptilian steeds known as Karkadraks or, in the rarest of cases, ascend to the ranks of the Varanguard – the chosen knights of Archaon himself.

The Slaves to Darkness are the unquestioned masters of the Bloodwind Spoil. Carngrad is theirs, as are many of the ruined fortresses and abandoned cities that lie scattered across the land. There is no overarching goal that defines their efforts in this place, save to ensure that Archaon's will is obeyed in all things. Warbands roam the Spoil on all manner of dark quests, as many and varied in scope and intent as the champions who lead them. Any who encounter them are liable to be put for the sword, if nothing more than for the brief sport they will provide these black-hearted warriors.

Since the breaching of the Shyishan arcway by the armies of Katakros, Mortarch of the Necropolis, the Varanguard have not been idle. What has happened once may happen again. So do the Knights of the Empty Throne, the Everchosen's innermost circle, ride across the Bloodwind Spoil in greater numbers than ever before. The champion of those warbands they encounter are soon slaughtered, their warriors bound to their service and brought to garrison the arcways connecting to Ghur and Chamon. Should any other fools seek to breach Archaon's domain, they will find the cost grave indeed.

SLAVES TO DARKNESS

The tribes of ruin have spread far and wide across the Mortal Realms. The warriors that throng the hordes of Chaos all seek to ascend the Path to Glory, pleasing the Dark Gods through acts of carnage and sacrifice in the pursuit of immortality and a dark apotheosis.

SLAVES TO DARKNESS FIGHTER ABILITIES

[Double] Imbued with Dark Power: Until the end of this fighter's activation, add the value of this ability to the Strength characteristic of attack actions made by this fighter that have a Range characteristic of 3 or less.

[Double] Throw Javelin: Pick a visible enemy fighter within 6" of this fighter and roll a dice. On a 3-4, allocate 1 damage point to that fighter. On a 5-6, allocate a number of damage points to that fighter equal to the value of this ability.

[Double] Shield Ram: Until the end of this fighter's activation, the next time this fighter finishes a move action within 1" of an enemy fighter, pick a visible enemy fighter within 1" of this fighter and roll a dice. On a 4-5, allocate 1 damage point to that fighter. On a 6, allocate a number of damage points to that fighter equal to the value of this ability.

[Triple] Trampling Hooves: Until the end of this fighter's activation, the next time this fighter finishes a move action within 1" of an enemy fighter, pick a visible enemy fighter within 1" of this fighter. Allocate a number of damage points to that fighter equal to the value of this ability.

[Quad] Lead the Slaughter: A fighter can use this ability only if an enemy fighter has been taken down by an attack action made by them this activation. Until the end of the battle round, add half the value of this ability (rounding up) to the Attacks characteristic of attack actions made by visible friendly fighters while they are within 6" of this fighter.

SLAVES TO DARKNESS LEADER ABILITIES

[Double] Daemonic Power: Pick a visible friendly fighter within 8" of this fighter. Until the end of the battle round, add 1 to the Strength and Attacks characteristics of the next attack action made by that fighter that has a Range characteristic of 3 or less.

[Double] Relentless Killers: Add half the value of this ability (rounding up) to the Attacks characteristic of the next attack action made by this fighter that has a Range characteristic of 3 or less.

[Triple] Spurred by the Gods: Until the end of the battle round, add 1 to the Attacks characteristic of attack actions that have a Range characteristic of 3 or less made by friendly fighters while they are within 3" of this fighter.

[Triple] Knights of Chaos: Until the end of the battle round, add 2 to the Move characteristic of friendly fighters with the **Mount** runemark () that start their activation within 6" of this fighter.

[Triple] Champion of Darkness: A fighter can use this ability only if an enemy fighter has been taken down by an attack action made by them this activation. This fighter makes a bonus move action. Then, they can make a bonus attack action.

[Quad] Deathblow: Add the value of this ability to the damage points allocated to enemy fighters by each hit or critical hit from the next attack action made by this fighter this activation that has a Range characteristic of 3 or less.

SLAVES TO DARKNESS SWORDBANDS

DARKOATH CHIEFTAIN — 190

⚔	1	4	4	2/5	

4 | 4 | 25

EXALTED HERO OF CHAOS — 230

🪓	1	5	4	2/5	

4 | 5 | 28

DARKOATH WARQUEEN — 195

🪓	1	3	4	2/4	

4 | 5 | 25

CHAOS SORCERER LORD — 165

⚡	3-7	2	3	3/6	
🔨		2	3	3	1/4

4 | 3 | 20

CHAOS LORD — 255

➤	2	5	5	3/5	

4 | 5 | 28

CHAOS LORD ON KARKADRAK — 310

➤	2	4	5	2/5	

8 | 6 | 38

CHAOS LORD ON DAEMONIC MOUNT — 295

🪓	1	5	4	2/4	

10 | 5 | 32

VARANGUARD
1 | 4 | 4 | 3/5

10 | 6 | 35

310

DOOM KNIGHT
2 | 4 | 4 | 2/4

10 | 6 | 32

285

EXALTED CHAMPION
2 | 5 | 5 | 3/5

4 | 5 | 28

250

MARAUDER CHIEFTAIN
1 | 4 | 4 | 2/5

4 | 3 | 20

140

ASPIRING CHAMPION
1 | 5 | 4 | 2/4

4 | 5 | 25

220

HORSEMASTER
1 | 3 | 4 | 2/5

10 | 4 | 30

225

CHAOS WARRIOR WITH CHAOS HAND WEAPON AND RUNESHIELD — 170

1	3	4	2/4

4 | 6 | 15

CHAOS MARAUDER WITH BARBARIAN AXE AND DARKWOOD SHIELD — 60

1	2	3	1/3

4 | 4 | 10

CHAOS WARRIOR WITH PAIR OF CHAOS HAND WEAPONS — 145

1	4	4	2/4

4 | 5 | 15

CHAOS MARAUDER HORSEMAN WITH MARAUDER FLAIL — 120

3	3	3	1/3

10 | 3 | 20

CHAOS WARRIOR WITH CHAOS HALBERD AND RUNESHIELD — 165

2	2	4	2/5

4 | 6 | 15

CHAOS MARAUDER HORSEMAN WITH AXE AND SHIELD — 125

1	2	3	1/3

10 | 4 | 20

CHAOS WARRIOR WITH CHAOS GREATBLADE — 170

1	3	5	3/5

4 | 5 | 15

CHAOS MARAUDER HORSEMAN WITH JAVELIN AND DARKWOOD SHIELD — 140

2	2	3	1/4

10 | 4 | 20

CHAOS CHOSEN — 180

1	4	5	2/5

4 | 5 | 18

CHAOS KNIGHT WITH CURSED LANCE AND CHAOS RUNESHIELD — 220

2	2	4	2/5

10 | 6 | 22

CHAOS MARAUDER WITH BARBARIAN FLAIL — 55

3	3	3	1/3

4 | 3 | 10

CHAOS KNIGHT WITH ENSORCELLED WEAPON AND CHAOS RUNESHIELD — 220

1	3	4	2/4

10 | 6 | 22

IRON GOLEM

The Iron Golems are master weaponsmiths who believe themselves destined to forge tools of destruction for Archaon's own legion. Those who face them must stand before peerless forgecraft and ironclad discipline alike.

The Ferrium Mountains of Chamon ring to the crash of hammers, the hiss of infernal forges and the march of armoured warriors. This is the claim of the Iron Golems, and they have won it with metal and with mettle alike. Their disciplined ranks march in search of conquest, each warrior proven in the testing crucible of war. To the Iron Golems, the flames of their furnaces are the true face of Chaos. These are stoked with the bodies of crushed enemies, an offering to the gods in steel and fire.

The citadel of the Iron Golems, Tharkar Zaal, dominates the Ferrium Mountains. Chemical ash floes streak down the mountains; those who do not succumb to the blights caused by this waste find their flesh growing hard and grey. Amongst the Iron Legion it is considered a rite of passage to withstand these chemical storms without complaint or grimace. Tharkar Zaal is as much a colossal forge as it is a fortress, and from its depths emerge an endless supply of war materiel fashioned from the natural resources of the Ferrium Mountains. The extractors of these resources are inevitably slaves, and if one wishes to treat with the Golems then mortal chattel – of which ogors are the most prized, starved and beaten until their minds shatter entirely – is a typical price. The Iron Legion garrisons many ports along the Alloy Ocean, trading with other Chaos warbands and tainted duardin forgelords to expand their own wealth.

'We create war.'

- Maxim of the Iron Golems

The greatest secret of the Golems lies beneath the Ferrium Mountains. Here is the prison of Axranathos, a monstrous Sun Dragon enslaved by the Iron Legion. The magma channels spewed by this beast are used to forge prized tools of war. Axranathos has broken free on several occasions, but like all enemies of the Golems, the dragon has been corralled by the redoubtable Iron Legionaries, assailed by storms of hurled bolas, and battered into submission by the uncompromising Drillmasters, champion Prefectors and veteran Dominar captains that command the Iron Golems.

It is said that Mithraxes, the current High Overlord of the Iron Golems, plots to send an expedition into the industrialised region of Angazkul-Grend that lies towards the foot of the Varanspire. By conquering and fortifying this land, and by ensuring that more hellish armaments leave its great forges than ever before, he believes that his place at Archaon's side will be assured. His champions lead their warbands to fight across the Bloodwind Spoil with redoubled fervour, each striving to prove worthy of leading this grand campaign.

IRON GOLEM ABILITIES

	[Double] Throw Bolas: Pick a visible enemy fighter within 6" of this fighter and roll 2 dice. For each roll of 4-5, allocate 1 damage point to that fighter. For each roll of 6, allocate a number of damage points to that fighter equal to the value of this ability.
	[Double] Spine-crushing Blow: Add the value of this ability to the Strength characteristic of the next attack action made by this fighter this activation that has a Range characteristic of 3 or less.
	[Double] Lead with Strength: A fighter can use this ability only if an enemy fighter has been taken down by an attack action made by them this activation. This fighter makes a bonus move action or a bonus attack action.
	[Triple] Living Battering Ram: Until the end of this fighter's activation, the next time this fighter finishes a move action within 1" of an enemy fighter, pick a visible enemy fighter within 1" of this fighter. Allocate a number of damage points to that fighter equal to the value of this ability.
	[Triple] Stand Defiant: Until the end of the battle round, add 1 to the Toughness characteristic of friendly fighters while they are within 6" of this fighter.
	[Quad] Whirlwind of Death: Allocate a number of damage points to all visible enemy fighters within 3" of this fighter equal to the value of this ability.

DOMINAR
🔨	↩	⚡	✊	🛡
1	3	5	2/5
➶ 4	☀ 4	💀 20		

175

DRILLMASTER
🔨	↩	⚡	✊	🛡
1	4	4	2/4
3	4	4	1/2
➶ 5	☀ 4	💀 15		

125

SIGNIFER
🔨	↩	⚡	✊	🛡
1	3	4	2/4
➶ 4	☀ 4	💀 15		

120

PREFECTOR
🔨	↩	⚡	✊	🛡
1	3	4	2/5
➶ 4	☀ 4	💀 15		

125

IRON LEGIONARY
🔨	↩	⚡	✊	🛡
1	2	3	1/3
➶ 4	☀ 5	💀 10		

80

ARMATOR
🔨	↩	⚡	✊	🛡
1	4	4	1/4
➶ 3	☀ 4	💀 12		

90

OGOR BREACHER
🐛	↩	⚡	✊	🛡
1	2	6	4/8
➶ 4	☀ 5	💀 30		

235

IRON LEGIONARY WITH BOLAS
⚓	↩	⚡	✊	🛡
3	3	3	1/2
1	2	3	1/3
➶ 4	☀ 4	💀 10		

65

IRON LEGIONARY WITH TWIN HAMMERS
🔨	↩	⚡	✊	🛡
1	3	3	1/3
➶ 4	☀ 4	💀 10		

70

UNTAMED BEASTS

Howling and roaring in praise to the Dark Gods, the Untamed Beasts tear across the plains with boundless ferocity. In all the realms, there are few worshippers of Chaos as savage as these veteran hunters.

To the Untamed Beasts, there is only one truth – all that is civilised and ordered is naught but prey. These nomadic hunters roam the Jagged Savannah of Ghur. Only the most brutal of predators could survive here – and the Untamed Beasts assuredly fall into this category.

The Untamed Beasts worship Chaos as the Devourer of Existence. They believe that everything forged by mortalkind – from there merest of metal dirks to the grandest city walls – is a meaningless foible destined to perish in the maw of this rapacious deity. Even other worshippers of Chaos are not immune to this; the Iron Golems in particular are despised for their industrious forgecraft, and the battles between these rival warbands are amongst the bloodiest to be found in all the Bloodwind Spoil. Only Archaon is above reproach, for he is the Eater of Worlds – the living incarnation of the Untamed Beasts' god – and it is he who will sound the blood-horns and call the Last Hunt. On that day the Untamed Beasts will fight at the forefront of his legions, tearing down all in their path so that the realms may be refashioned according to their own savage creed.

'Hunt the Hunter.'

- War-chant of the Untamed Beasts

The Untamed Beasts hunt predatory creatures alone, for they consider this the truest test of their skills. They wield weapons crafted from the claws and fangs of these animals, and erect temporary camps from their hides and bones. The Heart-eaters who lead the hunts are hulking chieftains who have devoured the organs of monsters and been bolstered by their primal essence. The honour of both commencing and concluding a kill, however, belongs to the First Fangs; these are the keenest eyes of the Untamed Beasts, whose javelins can bring down even the mightiest predators. Eager Plains-runners charge alongside grizzled Preytakers – veteran warriors who have slain mighty beasts and, in doing so, earned the right to choose for themselves a name. Perhaps the most honoured of the Untamed Beasts, however, are the Beastspeakers. These shamans are said to commune with the Devourer of Existence itself, and they direct the predators bound into service by the Untamed Beasts – the fierce Rocktusk Prowlers chief amongst them.

The Untamed Beasts and the Brayherds of the gor-kin share much in common. Indeed, the tribes of the Jagged Savannah are some of the only outsiders permitted to join the orgiastic blood-revels that rage around twisted Herdstones – though with the violent core that lurks within all these savage hunters, it is not surprising that internecine violence often breaks out anyway.

UNTAMED BEASTS ABILITIES	
	[Double] Savage Fury: Add 1 to the Move characteristic of this fighter for the next move action they make this activation, and add 1 to the Attacks characteristic of the next attack action they make this activation.
	[Double] All-out Attack: A fighter can use this ability only if an enemy fighter has been taken down by an attack action made by them this activation. This fighter makes a bonus move action or a bonus attack action.
	[Double] Beastmaster: Pick a visible friendly fighter with the **Beast** runemark (🐾) within 4" of this fighter. That fighter makes a bonus attack action.
	[Triple] Pounce: Until the end of this fighter's activation, the next time this fighter finishes a move action within 1" of an enemy fighter, pick a visible enemy fighter within 1" of this fighter. Allocate a number of damage points to that fighter equal to the value of this ability.
	[Triple] Harpoon Snag: This fighter makes a bonus attack action. After that attack action, the fighter targeted by that attack action makes a bonus move action directly towards this fighter, as if they were jumping, a number of inches equal to the value of this ability.
	[Quad] Unleash the Beast: Until the end of the battle round, add half the value of this ability (rounding up) to the Attacks and Strength characteristics of attack actions made by this fighter that have a Range characteristic of 3 or less.

HEART-EATER 180

	1	4	4	2/5

5 | 4 | 20

FIRST FANG 140

	8	2	4	2/5
	1	3	4	1/4

4 | 4 | 15

BEASTSPEAKER 125

	4	4	4	1/2
	1	3	4	1/4

5 | 4 | 15

ROCKTUSK PROWLER 180

	1	4	4	2/5

8 | 4 | 20

PREYTAKER WITH FANGED AXE 105

	1	3	4	2/4

4 | 4 | 10

PREYTAKER WITH SAWTOOTH BLADE 105

	1	4	3	2/4

4 | 4 | 10

PLAINS-RUNNER 55

	1	3	3	1/3

5 | 3 | 8

CORVUS CABAL

Striking from the shadows of Ulgu without warning or mercy, the Corvus Cabal are a cult of avaricious assassins. They favour descending from above with wicked war-picks flashing, slaughtering their prey with cruel precision.

When a corpse is found abandoned in the Cities of Sigmar with its eyes plucked out, its throat slit and its valuables stripped, then the Corvus Cabal are undeniably near. From the mist-shrouded mesas of Carrion Reach, hidden somewhere in the Ulguan Dominion of Klarondu, these sinister cultists stalk and slay without remorse any they deem a worthy target.

Carrion Reach is home to a wide variety of scavengers, birds in particular. They haunt the shadowy clefts and lurk amidst crooked trees, watching as offerings of flesh and gold are amassed by the Chaos-worshippers. It is after these beasts that the Cabal has modelled its worship of the Ruinous Powers. They pay homage to Chaos in the form of the Great Gatherer, a monstrous corvid whose black-feathered wings are wrapped in opulent chains and whose nest of bones drips with the blood of emperors and paupers alike. The Great Gatherer is a demanding god, and to appease its terrible hunger the Cabal must secure a constant tribute of stolen treasures. Those who fail to provide suitable offerings are hurled from the Throne of Vultures, the highest of Carrion Reach's many peaks, to be dashed into oblivion on the rocks below – their broken corpses swarmed and devoured by the avian children of the Gatherer.

'Pick clean the corpse.'

- Graffiti often found daubed in blood near the
Corvus Cabal's victims

Worship of the Great Gatherer has spread beyond Carrion Reach. In shadowed alleyways, cut-purses and thieves worship at secret shrines surrounded by animal bones and pilfered baubles. There are even those outwardly genial merchants who pay homage to the deity, whether out of jealousy for their rivals' wealth or desperation to defend their own. By offering trinkets dipped in blood to passing corvids, these faithful may attract the gaze of a Shadow Piercer – the mysterious leaders of the assassin flocks. Cabalists, Shadow Stalkers and nightmarish Shrike Talons are then dispatched to hunt down those the bargainer wishes dead. The Cabal will extract suitable reward from the bodies of the slain, but those who seek them out must also make a fine offering to the Gatherer – or it will be their entrails that come to decorate the offering-trees of the Cabal.

The distinctive razor-thorn shrines of the Corvus Cabal can be found across the Bloodwind Spoil, but the greatest are strung between the highest spires of Carngrad. It is from here that the Cabal control a host of roof-runner gangers, honing their aerial strikes so that when they attack, there is nothing the enemy can do but perish.

CORVUS CABAL ABILITIES

	[Double] Raven Dart: Pick a visible enemy fighter within 8" of this fighter and roll a dice. On a 3-5, allocate 1 damage point to that fighter. On a 6, allocate a number of damage points to that fighter equal to the value of this ability.
	[Double] Swift Climb: Until the end of this fighter's activation, do not count the vertical distance moved when this fighter is climbing.
	[Double] Harrying Raven: Pick an enemy fighter within 20" of this fighter. Until the end of the battle round, that fighter cannot make disengage actions.
	[Triple] Swooping Attack: This fighter makes a bonus move action. In addition, if the fighter finishes that move action 3" or more vertically lower than their starting position, they can make a bonus attack action.
	[Triple] Grisly Trophy: Until the end of the battle round, add 1 to the Attacks characteristic of attack actions that have a Range characteristic of 3 or less made by visible friendly fighters while they are within 6" of this fighter.
	[Quad] Death from Above: This fighter makes a bonus move action. Then, they can make a bonus attack action. Add 1 to the Strength characteristic of that attack action if the fighter finished the move action 3" or more vertically lower than their starting position.

SHADOW PIERCER — 185

⚔️	🏹	⚔️	✊	🛡️
1	4	4	2/5

🏹 5 ⚫ 4 💀 20

CABALIST — 65

⚔️	🏹	⚔️	✊	🛡️
1	4	3	1/3

🏹 5 ⚫ 3 💀 8

SHRIKE TALON — 175

🦅	🏹	⚔️	✊	🛡️
	1	5	4	2/4

🏹 8 ⚫ 4 💀 20

CABALIST WITH SPEAR — 75

🗡️	🏹	⚔️	✊	🛡️
2	4	3	1/4

🏹 5 ⚫ 3 💀 8

SPIRE STALKER — 140

⚔️	🏹	⚔️	✊	🛡️
1	4	4	2/4

🏹 5 ⚫ 4 💀 15

CABALIST WITH FAMILIAR — 60

🔨	🏹	⚔️	✊	🛡️
1	3	3	1/3

🏹 5 ⚫ 3 💀 8

CYPHER LORDS

Though the Cypher Lords maintain a veneer of enlightenment, in reality they are as corrupt as any brutish Marauder. These Hyshian nobles worship madness as the face of Chaos, and seek to unravel sanity wherever they go.

It is said that the brightest light is often the most blinding, and so it is with the Cypher Lords. Behind their concealing sun-ray masks, supposedly fashioned in honour of the Hyshian brilliance that glows across their home in Xintil, the lords of the ziggurat-city of Nochseed are disciples of evil. Madness is their weapon; they delight in confounding the senses of their adversaries, revelling in the perversion of typical Hyshian values – advancements in logic, truth-seeking and the like – before dispatching these foes with elegant curved blades.

As with the Cypher Lords themselves, Nochseed harbours many secrets. Outsiders know of the College of Mirrors, a famed martial academy in which the blademasters of the Cypher Lords train, as well as Nochseed Dreamvint – a potent narcotic secretly enjoyed by many Xintilian nobles, who remain unaware of its mind-unravelling properties. Even those who suspect the truth about the Cypher Lords tell conflicting stories. Some claim that cabals of Sphiranxes who escaped the Teclian purge make their lairs within the city, others that Mutalith beasts are chained in caverns beneath the library-domes and worshipped by the Cypher Lords as manifestations of madness. It is even said that the nine Quintescent Luminaries who rule Nochseed are no longer entirely human. Then again, perhaps all these tales are false – simply more misinformation intentionally spread by the cunning Cypher Lords.

'Let madness reign.'

- Secret greeting between Cypher Lords agents

The Cypher Lords are master manipulators, using thralls known as Mindbound to do their will. These enslaved warriors are controlled through the use of mystic thrall-stones marked with the rune of Nochseed, artefacts that allow the Thrallmasters and Luminates – those who have stared into the eye of madness itself – to not only direct their thralls but also to see as they see. Many who bear this brand do not even realise they are enacting the will of Nochseed. There are even some Chaos Lords who are so marked, their rampages engineered to spread pandemonium in line with the Cypher Lords' aims.

To fight the Cypher Lords is to face smoke and mirrors. These cultists intend to become the spymasters of Archaon's armies, and seek to prove themselves through the artful destruction of their enemies from many angles. Mindbound thralls seem to shift and shimmer like insubstantial phantoms, knocking their opponents entirely off guard and rendering them easy prey for the agile warriors of Nochseed, who deliver the killing strike always from the most unexpected direction.

CYPHER LORDS ABILITIES	
	[Double] Throwing Stars and Chakrams: Pick a visible enemy fighter within 6" of this fighter and roll 2 dice. For each roll of 4-5, allocate 1 damage point to that fighter. For each roll of 6, allocate a number of damage points to that fighter equal to the value of this ability.
	[Double] Acrobatic Leap: This fighter can fly when making move actions until the end of their activation; however, when flying, they cannot move vertically upwards more than 3".
	[Double] Low Sweeping Blow: Roll 1 dice for each visible enemy fighter within 2" of this fighter. On a 4-5, allocate 1 damage point to the fighter being rolled for. On a 6, allocate a number of damage points to the fighter being rolled for equal to the value of this ability.
	[Triple] Shadowy Recall: Pick a friendly fighter with the **Minion** runemark (✧) that is within 12" of this fighter. Remove that fighter from the battlefield and then immediately set them up anywhere on the battlefield within a number of inches of this fighter equal to the value of this ability.
	[Triple] Shattered Gloom Globe: Until the end of the battle round, subtract 1 from the Attacks characteristic (to a minimum of 1) of attack actions made by enemy fighters while they are within 6" of this fighter.
	[Quad] Spinning Somersault Strike: This fighter can fly when making move actions until the end of their activation; however, when flying, they cannot move vertically upwards more than 3". In addition, this fighter makes a bonus move action. Then, they can make a bonus attack action.

THRALLMASTER — 205

5 · 4 · 20

MIRRORBLADE WITH DUELLING SWORDS — 115

5 · 3 · 10

LUMINATE — 175

5 · 4 · 15

MINDBOUND — 75

5 · 3 · 10

MIRRORBLADE WITH GLAIVE — 120

5 · 3 · 10

MINDBOUND WITH DOUBLE-BLADED SWORD — 80

5 · 3 · 10

THE UNMADE

The Unmade number amongst the most horrific of all worshippers of the Ruinous Powers. These savages mutilate themselves with the same vigour they do their foes, for they believe that pain is a gift they must share with all.

The Unmade live up to their name well. Beneath banners stitched from still-screaming faces and wearing crowns of living flesh, these sadists practise the grisly rites of unmaking – flaying their own flesh and hacking off limbs to replace them with wicked agonising weapons. As an Unmade rises from the ranks of the Awakened to the Ascended, the Joyous and finally the Blissful Ones, they cast off more and more of their humanity – the better to bring the purest pain to their hapless foes.

The philosopher-kings of Tzlid, an island within Shyish's Prime Innerlands, were once renowned across the Realm of Death for their nobility and wisdom. Greatest of them all was the heroic King Vourneste, yet his rule coincided with the kingdom's darkest days. The black forests of Tzlid were haunted by flesh-eating mordants, who devoured Vourneste's people and despoiled his lands. The king fought many great battles and earned several crushing victories over the cannibal hordes, but their numbers were great and his armies diminished with every campaign. Desperate, King Vourneste prayed for salvation – and was answered.

'Agony is our gift.'

- First Commandment of the Flayed Prince

In a dream, Vourneste saw the image of an ancient gate of rune-marked obsidian, beyond which lay his people's salvation. Gathering his greatest warriors, the king travelled into the depths of the forest, and there came upon the gateway from his vision. What transpired beyond that cursed gate remains a mystery, but when Vourneste emerged he had changed beyond recognition. His flesh was now festooned with barbed and serrated hooks. His skin hung in tatters from the ruins of his gleaming armour. His royal guard had been similarly mutilated, and marched silently behind their liege, blood dripping from their tortured flesh. That which had been Vourneste was dead, the monarch claimed, but the Flayed Prince would lead his people to victory.

The thing that had been Vourneste led his flock in vile ceremonies in which pain was embraced as a benediction. The people of Tzlid became the Unmade, grotesque raiders who stalked the darkness and stole away sacrifices for their great festivals of agony. It is said that the Flayed Prince was eventually slain at the hand of the Mortarch Neferata, though some of the Unmade believe he lives still. Many, however, instead see Archaon as a successor to their fallen master. Warbands of the Unmade regularly embark on pilgrimages to the court of the Everchosen, all seeking to earn a place in Archaon's legions and share the gift of pain with the realms at large.

THE UNMADE ABILITIES	
	[Double] Nightmarish Visage: Pick an enemy fighter within a number of inches of this fighter equal to the value of this ability and roll a dice. On a 3+, until the end of the battle round, that fighter cannot make move actions or disengage actions.
	[Double] Barbed Strike: Until the end of this fighter's activation, if any attack action made by this fighter scores any hits or critical hits, subtract 1 from the Toughness characteristic (to a minimum of 1) of the target fighter until the end of the battle round.
	[Double] Chain Garrotte: Pick an enemy fighter within 5" of this fighter and roll a dice. On a 3-4, allocate 1 damage point to that fighter. On a 5-6, allocate a number of damage points to that fighter equal to the value of this ability.
	[Triple] Flaying Frenzy: Roll a dice for each visible enemy fighter within 3" of this fighter. On a 3-4, allocate 1 damage point to the fighter being rolled for. On a 5-6, allocate a number of damage points to the fighter being rolled for equal to the value of this ability.
	[Triple] Vessel of Torment: A fighter can use this ability only if an enemy fighter has been taken down by an attack action made by them this activation. This fighter makes a bonus move action. Then, they can make a bonus attack action.
	[Quad] Gift of Agony: This fighter makes a bonus attack action. Add 1 to the Strength and Attacks characteristics of that attack action if this fighter has any damage points allocated to them.

BLISSFUL ONE · 220

🗡	↺ 1	⚡ 5	👊 4	🛡 2/6	

↗ 8 · ⊛ 4 · 💀 20

AWAKENED ONE WITH FLAIL · 60

⛓	↺ 3	⚡ 3	👊 3	🛡 1/2
🗡	↺ 1	⚡ 3	👊 3	🛡 1/3

↗ 4 · ⊛ 3 · 💀 10

JOYOUS ONE · 145

🗡	↺ 1	⚡ 4	👊 4	🛡 2/4	

↗ 5 · ⊛ 4 · 💀 15

ASCENDED ONE · 125

🗡	↺ 1	⚡ 4	👊 4	🛡 2/4

↗ 4 · ⊛ 4 · 💀 10

AWAKENED ONE WITH BRUTAL POLEARM · 60

➤	↺ 2	⚡ 2	👊 3	🛡 1/4

↗ 4 · ⊛ 3 · 💀 10

SPLINTERED FANG

Unlike many warrior cults, the Splintered Fang does not see the use of poison as a stain on their honour. Indeed, it is their favoured tool of war, their blades toxic enough to bring down even a gargant with several well-placed blows.

It is said that in ancient days, Ignax the Solar Drake battled Nagendra, Father of Serpents, in an apocalyptic clash that cracked the earth and boiled the seas. Ultimately the Solar Drake triumphed, tearing the hide of Nagendra apart with flaming talons. From his torn flesh grew venomous pit-coilers and immense constrictors – indeed, all the serpents of the realms.

The warriors of the Splintered Fang descend from the tribes of the great jungles of Invidia. These tribes worshipped Nagendra as part of a pantheon of animalistic spirit-deities, seeing the Father of Serpents as the embodiment of cunning and the patron of patient hunters. Over the centuries, that primal totemism was corrupted by Chaos. A growing sect calling themselves the Splintered Fang came to regard Nagendra as a malevolent predator that would one day rise from its long slumber to consume all things. Their shamans claimed to hear the voice of the sleeping serpent, but in fact it was the whispers of deceitful daemons that named themselves the Coiling Ones, promising untold power in exchange for the souls of unbelievers.

'One cut. One kill.'

- Prime Tenet of the Splintered Fang

One by one, the Splintered Fang killed the faithful tribes of the Invidian Pantheon. Some they pierced with poisoned blades, others they hurled into serpent-filled pits. Those that survived were acknowledged as Nagendra's Chosen, and given the honour of joining the Splintered Fang. Few refused, for the alternative was a horrific death. Over the centuries, the Splintered Fang grew in size and influence; their shamans demanded ever more sacrifices to appease the Coiling Ones, and so the serpent-worshippers constructed fighting pits and gladiatorial chambers into which they hurled their prisoners. Those that died were meat for the Father of Serpents, and those who thrived became his favoured champions – their blood inured to the venoms of his children, their weapons laced with his agonising gifts.

The Splintered Fang favour blades designed for stabbing and barbed, toxin-laced nets, the better to deliver the poisons brewed by the Serpent Callers – shamans of the Coiling Ones – into the bloodstream of their foes. They strike swiftly and score telling blows, then step back and circle their prey, allowing the poisons to do their work. Victims die in agony, their flesh swelling and their blood curdling like spoiled milk. Some are stricken by ophidian mutations, as fangs and jagged scales burst from their bones before their skin sloughs away to leave nothing but a malformed, mewling heap of flesh.

SPLINTERED FANG ABILITIES	
	[Double] Poisoned Weapon: Until the end of this fighter's activation, the Strength characteristic of attack actions made by this fighter count as being higher than the target's Toughness characteristic.
	[Double] Ensnaring Net: Pick a visible enemy fighter within 3" of this fighter. Until the end of the battle round, that enemy fighter cannot make move actions or disengage actions.
	[Double] Fanged Buckler: Pick a visible enemy fighter within 1" of this fighter and roll a dice. On a 3-4, allocate 1 damage point to that fighter. On a 5-6, allocate a number of damage points to that fighter equal to the value of this ability.
	[Triple] Snake Charmer: Pick a friendly fighter with the **Beast** runemark (🐍) within 4" of this fighter. That fighter makes a bonus attack action.
	[Triple] Relentless Killer: A fighter can use this ability only if an enemy fighter has been taken down by an attack action made by them this activation. This fighter makes a bonus attack action.
	[Quad] Paralysing Venom: Until the end of this fighter's activation, add the value of this ability to the damage points allocated by critical hits from attack actions made by this fighter, and after each attack action made by this fighter, roll a dice. On a 5-6, until the end of the battle round, the target fighter cannot make move actions or disengage actions.

TRUEBLOOD · 180

VENOMBLOOD WITH DUELLING BLADES · 85

SERPENT CALLER · 145

VENOMBLOOD WITH BLADE AND BARBED WHIP · 85

SERPENTS · 65

CLEARBLOOD · 65

PUREBLOOD · 125

CLEARBLOOD WITH SHIELD · 70

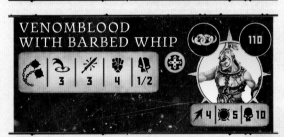
VENOMBLOOD WITH BARBED WHIP · 110

VENOMBLOOD WITH SPEAR AND SHIELD · 135

SCIONS OF THE FLAME

Even amongst the followers of the Ruinous Powers, the Scions of the Flame are zealots. These warriors worship the darkest fires of Aqshy, bringing their blazing wrath to bear on all they deem their enemies.

Hailing from the Great Parch of Aqshy, the Scions of the Flame are wild-eyed fanatics who worship Chaos as the Ever-Raging Flame. Fire is their weapon of choice, and those who stand before them are liable to be consumed by raging infernos or struck down by the blazing brazier-weapons wielded by this fearsome cult.

The epicentre of the Scions' blazing faith can be found in the Bright Mountains of Aspiria, an ash-choked stretch of volcanic peaks under which run sulphurous caverns and magma flows. Their temples are fortresses of bronze and flame that guard deposits of Aqshian realmstone – the deadly substance known by scholars of such matters as aqthracite. This realmstone is believed by the Scions to be the essence of the Ever-Raging Flame, and they guard it with single-minded fervour, gladly sacrificing their own lives by the hundred to keep avaricious raiders from laying claim to a single ember. Entire wars have been fought between the Scions and the Tzeentchian cabals that lurk in the ruins of the Agloraxi Empire over possession of aqthracite, both sides seeking to capture veins of the realmstone for their own diabolical ends.

'The flame within.'

- Element of the Scions' ritualistic chants

When sufficient quantities of aqthracite are gathered, the Scions of the Flame employ it in dark rituals to create volcanic upheaval across vast stretches of the realms, drowning regions beneath tides of bubbling magma. The ash daemons who claim to be manifestations of the Ever-Raging Flame maintain that the realms must be drowned one and all in flaming doom, and it is this apocalyptic end that the Scions fight to bring about.

To truly enact the will of the Ever-Raging Flame, the cult requires vast quantities of realmstone, far more than they possess. Aqshy is the most lucrative source of aqthracite, but over the centuries many relics containing realmstone have ended up in the Eightpoints, either as spoils captured by conquering armies or as elements in the sinister schemes of sorcerers. So it is that the Blazing Lords lead to the Bloodwind Spoil warbands of zealous priests, burning champions and initiates seeking to pass through the flames of combat and be reborn as fearsome Fireborn. Even as they strive to earn their place in Archaon's armies they are forever seeking new sources of aqthracite, and will fight ferociously to capture the realmstone and further their cult's mission of annihilation.

SCIONS OF THE FLAME ABILITIES

	[Double] Fiery Might: Until the end of this fighter's activation, add half the value of this ability (rounding up) to the Strength characteristic of attack actions made by this fighter that have a Range characteristic of 3 or less.
	[Double] Beheading Strike: Add half the value of this ability (rounding up) to the damage points allocated by critical hits from the next attack action made by this fighter this activation that has a Range characteristic of 3 or less.
	[Double] Throw Fire Bomb: Pick a visible enemy fighter within 6" of this fighter and roll 2 dice. For each 4-5, allocate 1 damage point to that fighter. For each 6, allocate a number of damage points to that fighter equal to the value of this ability.
	[Triple] Inferno: Roll 1 dice for each visible enemy fighter within 3" of this fighter. On a 4-5, allocate 1 damage point to the fighter being rolled for. On a 6, allocate a number of damage points to the fighter being rolled for equal to the value of this ability.
	[Triple] Ignited Fervour: Until the end of the battle round, add 1 to the Attacks characteristic of attack actions that have a Range characteristic of 3 or less made by friendly fighters while they are within 6" of this fighter.
	[Quad] Engulf in Flames: Pick a visible enemy fighter within 3" of this fighter and roll 6 dice. For each 2+, allocate a number of damage points to that fighter equal to half the value of this ability (rounding up). In addition, for each 6, roll 1 extra dice as above (and so on).

BLAZING LORD — 190

2	4	5	2/6	

4 / 4 / 20

IMMOLATOR — 145

1	4	4	2/5	

4 / 4 / 15

BRAZEN CHAMPION — 170

2	3	5	3/6	

4 / 4 / 18

INFERNO PRIEST — 130

5	2	3	2/4	
2	3	4	2/4	

4 / 4 / 15

INITIATE WITH BRAZIER WEAPON — 65

1	3	4	1/3	

4 / 3 / 10

FIREBORN — 120

1	4	4	2/4	

4 / 4 / 10

INITIATE WITH FLAMEBURST POT — 55

1	3	3	1/3	

4 / 3 / 10

FIREBORN WITH SUNBLADE AND BRAZIER AXE — 115

1	4	4	2/4	

4 / 4 / 10

INITIATE WITH MORNING STAR — 55

3	3	3	1/3	

4 / 3 / 10

FIREBORN WITH SUNBLADE AND KRIS — 115

1	4	3	2/5	

4 / 4 / 10

INITIATE WITH HOOKED AXE — 65

1	4	3	1/3	

4 / 3 / 10

SPIRE TYRANTS

The Spire Tyrants are the champions of the blood pits of the Varanspire, fell-handed gladiators who exult in the goriest kills. They roam the Bloodwind Spoil as deadly packs, testing their blades against all they encounter.

Unlike many of the warbands who roam the Bloodwind Spoil, the Spire Tyrants do not originally hail from any one realm or culture. They are the champions of the Varanspire fighting pits, ferocious gladiators whose lives are dominated by the baying of the blood-hungry crowd. To thrive amongst the Spire Tyrants is to become a merciless butcher. They wield hardy, well-forged weapons and armour, gifts from patrons or trophies stripped from the corpses of defeated foes.

Even the blood and thunder of the arena ceases to hold any allure for such warriors. Instead, they seek greater tests, venturing out into the lethal wilds of the Eightpoints in search of worthy foes. Each desires to join the retinue of a Chaos warlord, perhaps even to wrest a place in the Everchosen's legions. But even a scarred veteran of the fighting pits does not easily win such an honour. It would require an offering of incredible power, a sacrifice worthy of the Three-Eyed King, in order to secure patronage. Those champions who dared approach one of Archaon's lieutenants without such a prize to display would meet a swift and bloody end.

'We are His chosen.'

- Creed of the Spire Tyrants

In the fighting pits of the Varanspire there are no such concepts as honour or valour, and all that matters is that one's foe is slain as spectacularly as possible for the entertainment of the howling audience. The theatricality of the arena is reflected in the combat style of these brutal warriors, who favour gory, drawn-out dismemberment over the quick and subtle kill. Potential patrons observing the death games demand more than simple bloodshed – they seek true artists of slaughter, gladiators that can show them horrors to quicken even their jaded, blackened hearts. More than that, the Spire Tyrants fight with the spiteful cunning of a Snarlfang pack, and know that even the fiercest opponents can have their will shattered after witnessing such horrendous violence meted out upon their finest warriors.

Spire Tyrant warbands are bound together not through ethnicity, gender or even race, but a desire to seek out and revel in the greatest of kills. Each gladiator favours their own idiosyncratic wargear and fighting style to triumph over their enemies and shame their rivals alike. From the bloody-handed champions of the pits to savage gor-kin, crazed duardin and cruel headsmen, those who face the Spire Tyrants on the plains of the Bloodwind Spoil can be certain of only one thing – death is coming from them, and it will be delivered in the most brutal fashion imaginable.

SPIRE TYRANTS ABILITIES	
	[Double] Pit Fighter: A fighter can use this ability only if an enemy fighter has been taken down by an attack action made by them this activation. This fighter can make a bonus move action or a bonus attack action.
	[Double] Gladiator's Net: Pick a visible enemy fighter within 3" of this fighter and roll 1 dice. On a 3+, that fighter cannot make move actions or disengage actions this battle round.
	[Double] Shield Ram: Until the end of this fighter's activation, the next time this fighter finishes a move action, pick a visible enemy fighter within 1" of this fighter and roll 1 dice. On a 4-5, allocate 1 damage point to that fighter. On a 6, allocate a number of damage points to that fighter equal to the value of this ability.
	[Triple] Readied Stance: Until the end of the battle round, add half the value of this ability (rounding up) to the Toughness characteristic of this fighter.
	[Triple] Champion of the Warpits: A fighter can use this ability only if an enemy fighter has been taken down by an attack action made by them this activation. Until the end of the battle round, add 1 to the Attacks characteristic of attack actions made by visible friendly fighters within 6" of this fighter.
	[Quad] Brutal Strike: Pick a visible enemy fighter within 1" of this fighter and roll 1 dice. On a 3-4, allocate a number of damage points to that fighter equal to the value of this ability. On a 5-6, allocate a number of damage points to that fighter equal to double the value of this ability.

PIT CHAMPION — 180

🗡	1	4	5	2/5
⚔	3	3	4	1/3

4 | 4 | 20

PIT FIGHTER WITH NET — 55

🗡	1	3	3	1/3

4 | 3 | 10

HEADCLAIMER — 135

🪓	1	3	5	2/5

4 | 4 | 15

PIT VETERAN WITH SHIELD — 110

🗡	1	2	3	2/4

4 | 5 | 10

BESTIGOR DESTROYER — 145

🔨	1	2	5	3/6

4 | 4 | 18

PIT VETERAN WITH DUAL WEAPONS — 105

🗡	1	3	3	2/4

4 | 4 | 10

PIT FIGHTER WITH PUNCH DAGGER — 60

🔨	1	4	3	1/3

4 | 3 | 10

FRENZIED RAGER — 95

🗡	1	4	4	1/4

3 | 4 | 12

PIT FIGHTER WITH SPEAR — 60

🔱	2	3	3	1/4

4 | 3 | 10

NARRATIVE PLAY

The rules presented in this section offer a whole host of additional narrative play content for all Chaos warbands in Warcry.

Four new fated quests will send your warband on new and twisted adventures, battling a host of foes to earn glory and reward in the eyes of the gods. A series of naming tables will allow you to further personalise your servants of the Ruinous Powers, fleshing out their personalities as they forge diabolic deals and overcome infernal challenges in the pursuit of ultimate power.

Also included in this section are six new challenge battles to add additional flavour to your campaigns. Each of these scenarios will test your wit and guile to the limits; those who prove worthy to the challenge will establish themselves as true champions of the Bloodwind Spoil, and earn powerful rewards to boot.

'Power belongs to those who can take it. Glory is won by those whose names are known to the gods.'

BEASTS OF CHAOS

Savage and anarchic, the Beasts of Chaos seek to tear civilisation apart. Even the lightest concession to society and law infuriates these creatures, awakening in them a bestial killing rage.

The Beasts of Chaos have long dwelt in the wild places of the Mortal Realms. Even during the Age of Myth these creatures menaced the civilised lands, and their alliance with the primal essence of anarchy has only made them more deadly. Their marauding Greatfrays contain all manner of bestial warriors; the cunning gor-kin of the Brayherds are master ambushers, while the brutes of the Warherds are cursed with an insatiable bloodgreed. Warring alongside them are the Dragon Ogors, ancient inhabitants of Azyr banished by the God-King and empowered by the touch of lightning.

BEASTS OF CHAOS FIRST NAMES	
D10	**NAME**
1	Ghorak
2	Surlok
3	Kraggahagh
4	Odogor
5	Darvik
6	Vosgar
7	Jakka
8	Azavak
9	Horgaros
10	Azgathor

BEASTS OF CHAOS LAST NAMES	
D10	**NAME**
1	Blood-Horn
2	the Flesh-Hungry
3	Fangmaw
4	the Warped
5	Mantearer
6	Gorepelt
7	Wrathfang
8	the Trampler
9	Wildkin
10	Stormgorged

ORIGIN	
1	**Furious Despoilers** – Your warband never misses a chance to wreak havoc upon even the crudest forms of civilisation.
2	**Dream Visions** – A Bray-Shaman's prophetic visions have foreseen a great destiny for your warband.
3	**Champions of the Warped Wild** – Your warband has long roamed the plains of the Eightpoints, wreaking terror across the blasted land.
4	**Masterful Stalkers** – Your warband excels at launching blistering ambushes upon the unwary.
5	**Propagators of Devolution** – Your warband seeks to reduce all to a primordial sludge of raw Chaos.
6	**Children of the Gods** – Your warriors have sworn themselves to one of the great powers of Chaos.

LEADER/FAVOURED WARRIOR BACKGROUND	
1	**Prince amongst Predators** – This beast controls its warriors through a brutal animalistic charisma.
2	**Ear-splitting Howl** – This warrior's battle roar can utterly deafen those nearby.
3	**Eater of Heroes** – This warrior hungers for the flesh of the mightiest champions.
4	**Excessive Violence** – The violence unleashed by this warrior leaves little of their prey intact.
5	**Ancient Terror** – This warrior has lived for many long centuries and has learnt countless ways to slaughter the foe.
6	**Lord of Storms** – Tainted lightning constantly flickers around this storm-touched warrior.

BLADES OF KHORNE

Khorne is a wrathful god, the oldest and most ferocious of the Ruinous Powers. His sole desire is to plunge all of creation into a ceaseless state of brutal bloodshed.

Many mortals have devoted themselves to Khorne, for the Lord of Skulls offers great boons to those who kill in his name. These warriors – known as the Bloodbound – are savage fighters, revelling in bloodshed no matter who falls beneath their axes. Should the Bloodbound slay enough to fray the fabric of reality, then the daemons of Khorne may burst through the veil. These terrifying apparitions are deadly beyond belief, their entire being shaped by mortal hatred and rage. They seek out the greatest enemies to destroy, particularly the followers of indulgent Slaanesh, who Khorne despises above all others.

BLADES OF KHORNE FIRST NAMES	
D10	NAME
1	Karthax
2	Vrasahk
3	Arbaal
4	Vorga
5	Gharvax
6	Khorrek
7	Tarkal
8	Ashkhos
9	Horkhos
10	Damakhar

BLADES OF KHORNE LAST NAMES	
D10	NAME
1	Ragemarrow
2	Skullcleave
3	Neckrend
4	Gorebringer
5	the Death of Honour
6	Kinslayer
7	Furyfang
8	Spineshatter
9	Mangouge
10	the Red Pilgrim

ORIGIN	
1	**Warriors of the Bright Realm** – These warriors have fought extensively in the fiery realm of Aqshy.
2	**An Axe to Grind** – Your warband seeks to utterly destroy an old rival.
3	**Red Headsmen** – These warriors pride themselves on slaying their foes with a single decapitating strike.
4	**Gorged on Gore** – In the aftermath of battle, your warband drinks deep of the spilled lifeblood of the foe.
5	**Destroy the Cowardly** – Your warriors have a special loathing for those who do not engage them in honourable battle.
6	**Bane of the Eldritch** – Since the dawning of the Arcanum Optimar, these warriors have made a point of hunting down and slaying wielders of magic.

LEADER/FAVOURED WARRIOR BACKGROUND	
1	**Scarred by War** – This warrior's many, many scars speak to a lifetime of conflict and bloodshed.
2	**Khorne Cares Not** – This warrior has slaughtered many of their own followers in the Blood God's name.
3	**Gift of Brass** – This warrior's skin, or even blood, glows like molten brass.
4	**Echoes of the Red Century** – This warrior favours testing themselves against the servants of other Chaos powers.
5	**Infernal Champion** – It is said that this warrior has triumphed over a mighty daemonic Herald of the Blood God in one-on-one combat.
6	**Never Stop! Never Tire!** – This warrior refuses to let a day go by without slaying something in Khorne's name.

DISCIPLES OF TZEENTCH

Tzeentch is the Chaos God of change, lies and sorcery. His plots span across all of creation, and he is empowered by the false hopes of mortals. Whether sinister cultist, savage Tzaangor or cackling daemon, the servants of Tzeentch are amongst the most bizarre devotees of Chaos.

Tzeentch's minions revel in manipulation – after all, it is not for nothing that their patron is known as the Architect of Fate. Within great cities lurk hidden Kairic Acolytes, while vicious Tzaangor flocks stalk the warped wilds. The daemons of Tzeentch are especially strange, often casting forth gouts of aetheric fire. Tzeentch is the greatest patron of sorcery among the Chaos Gods, and so it is little surprise that many of his followers are mighty wizards, their sorcerous power rewriting the very laws of reality.

DISCIPLES OF TZEENTCH FIRST NAMES		DISCIPLES OF TZEENTCH LAST NAMES	
D10	**NAME**	**D10**	**NAME**
1	Paralax	1	Xalarap
2	Vyzorak	2	P'teimus
3	Ocladius	3	Shimmer-Twist
4	Iridios	4	Xamolomax
5	Zirithinion	5	the Burning Jester
6	Ak'glar	6	R'tecfar
7	Kleok	7	Quiverbloom
8	Morax'nar	8	Zxyrtx
9	Shrixgyrl	9	Thalamyr
10	Virikizzik	10	Inkineilis

	ORIGIN		LEADER/FAVOURED WARRIOR BACKGROUND
1	**To the Master's Tune** – Your warband is entangled in a complex web of plots and schemes.	1	**Cackling Maniac** – Even by the standards of Tzeentch's servants, this warrior is truly mad.
2	**The Hidden Threat** – Your warriors lurk amidst enemy territory, waiting for the perfect moment to strike.	2	**Wheels within Wheels** – This warrior is particularly adept at manipulating others to serve their will.
3	**Seeking Ascension** – Your warriors wish to transmute into new and wondrous forms – or have done so already.	3	**Child of Flux** – This warrior seeks new mutations, no matter how impractical, with a rabid devotion.
4	**A Foolish Pact** – Your warband once made an alliance with a local warlord, but you have long since betrayed them for personal gain. No doubt they seek revenge even now.	4	**Esoteric Obsession** – This warrior hoards knowledge, both mystical and mundane, with an utterly deranged conviction.
5	**Duplicitous** – Your warriors delight in spreading confusion and misrule wherever they go.	5	**A Wicked Jest** – This warrior has a cruel sense of humour and delights in tormenting their foes with traps and illusions.
6	**Pyromaniacal** – These warriors seek to bring Tzeentch's flickering fires to all they encounter.	6	**Wreathed in Warpflame** – Coruscating changefire swirls around this warrior, occasionally manifesting into short-lived daemonic imps.

MAGGOTKIN OF NURGLE

Nurgle's power waxes whenever sickness and despair stalk the land. Yet despite the misery his 'gifts' spread, the Lord of Plagues is seen as a jovial, almost loving god, doting upon his warriors as if they were his rancid children.

Nurgle's obsession with the cycle of life and death – reflected in the foetid Garden that forms his domain in the Realm of Chaos – has seen him infect the Mortal Realms with all manner of hideous, virulent diseases. Those mortals who accept these dubious gifts become known as Rotbringers: bloated, fleshy monsters that are nearly impossible to slay. Marching by their side are the daemonic legions of Grandfather Nurgle. From maudlin Plaguebearers to giggling Nurglings, these beings revel in foulness, and wherever they tread the land will be blighted for years to come.

MAGGOTKIN OF NURGLE FIRST NAMES	
D10	**NAME**
1	Bolgarax
2	Prosternox
3	Skabius
4	Gluttoch
5	Felch
6	Skurvus
7	Kankerous
8	Ogblort
9	Wolgus
10	Gangrenous

MAGGOTKIN OF NURGLE LAST NAMES	
D10	**NAME**
1	Witherwort
2	Bilebelch
3	Poxmolion
4	Rustdrool
5	Rancodiox
6	Seepling
7	Festerfane
8	the Droning One
9	Maggatakus
10	Pusdrool

	ORIGIN
1	**Vectors of Contagion** – Your warriors are infected with a new and virulent form of disease fresh from Nurgle's cauldron.
2	**Letting the Garden Grow** – Your warband wishes to see Nurgle's Garden flourish across the realms.
3	**Spreading the Love** – Your warband measures their success by the number of mortals they have blessed with Nurgle's 'gifts'.
4	**Grandfather's Favoured** – Your warband is patronised by a powerful rot-daemon, who dotes on them like beloved children.
5	**Hatred of Purity** – This warband seeks out the most noble of foes to corrupt and despoil.
6	**The Cycle of Life** – Your warriors are obsessed with propagating Nurgle's gruesome cycle, wishing to see all wither before being reborn in fouler form.

	LEADER/FAVOURED WARRIOR BACKGROUND
1	**Jolly** – This warrior is surprisingly gregarious as they go about their disgusting business.
2	**Beloved Pets** – A writhing carpet of maggots and fat-bodied flies crawls over this warrior's body.
3	**Dolorous** – This warrior is filled with Nurgle's blessed despair.
4	**Droning Doom** – This warrior speaks eternally in maudlin rhyme.
5	**Truly Revolting** – Where this warrior walks, the realms themselves seem to wither and rot.
6	**Irascible** – This warrior has no patience for any who would impede their mission to spread decay or disease.

HEDONITES OF SLAANESH

Slaanesh, the Dark Prince, is the youngest of the Chaos Gods. His spheres are excess, indulgence and obsession, and every sensation felt to a great extent fuels this hungering deity.

For many long centuries, Slaanesh has languished in a prison created by the aelven gods. In his absence, his mortal worshippers and daemonic servants have continued their mission to spread depravity across the realms. Be they ambitious Pretenders seeking to replace the Dark Prince, relentless Godseekers hunting down their lord, or the simply war-hungry maniacs of the Invaders, Hedonites are a common sight in the Eightpoints. They travel at a swift pace, cackling madly as they indulge their dark fancies, sharp claws and elegant blades bringing agonising yet blissful death to those who cross their path.

HEDONITES OF SLAANESH FIRST NAMES	
D10	**NAME**
1	Daraetha
2	Sslithian
3	Tarmelion
4	Mytheira
5	Zirocoa
6	Oulakan
7	Marquaelis
8	Lathanshar
9	Terashon
10	Azaraen

HEDONITES OF SLAANESH LAST NAMES	
D10	**NAME**
1	Sybilath
2	Luxsion
3	Heartslake
4	Sinsate
5	Blisshowl
6	Mhal Pr'athis
7	Vyoresha
8	Gy'atha
9	Quiverthrash
10	Lyssimir

ORIGIN	
1	**Devoted** – These warriors wholeheartedly believe their leader to be Slaanesh's rightful heir – perhaps even a reincarnation of the god.
2	**Egomaniacs** – Each member of this warband considers themselves to be the finest of all warriors.
3	**On the Hunt** – Your warriors tirelessly hunt for their lost god, never halting in the chase and ruthlessly torturing those they capture for information.
4	**Ecstatic Desecrators** – Your warriors desire nothing more than to spread corruption, to see all that was once righteous rendered perverse and vile.
5	**Devotees of the Screaming Coil** – Your warband is on a winding pilgrimage to the Screaming Coil, believing the ancient device to be a relic of their god.
6	**A Contest of Blades** – Your warriors compete amongst themselves to inflict the most debilitating wounds on their foes without killing them outright.

LEADER/FAVOURED WARRIOR BACKGROUND	
1	**Heir to the Sinful Throne** – This warrior believes that they alone are destined to take up Slaanesh's mantle.
2	**Out of Favour** – This warrior was once a Herald or warleader amongst their Host, and schemes to reclaim their former glory once more.
3	**Alluring** – Those who face this warrior are struck dumb by their loathsome and strange beauty.
4	**Perfectionist** – This warrior is obsessed with delivering perfect strikes, and will fly into a petulant – but deadly – rage should they kill with anything less than the utmost artistry.
5	**Hedonistic Exemplar** – This warrior is fanatically devoted to a particular form of vice.
6	**Wicked Wit** – The insults hurled by this warrior are creative enough to make even an ogor blush.

SKAVEN

Cunning and malevolent, the skaven seek to spread ruin and corruption wherever they go. This insidious race of vermin-men worships the foul god known as the Great Horned Rat, and their plots and schemes are truly diabolical in their complexity.

Every skaven is egotistical and self-absorbed in the extreme; each fully believes in their own supremacy, and that all contenders must be destroyed to secure their position. Organised into different clans, each specialising in a different method of death, these ratmen will take any opportunity to claw their way to the top of the pecking order. All skaven must constantly be on guard against their underlings, for though they are not brave, they are vicious opportunists – and the lands of the Eightpoints are a fine place to organise 'accidents' for their rivals.

SKAVEN FIRST NAMES	
D10	**NAME**
1	Kretch
2	Niritik
3	Ratch
4	Grask
5	Rikkit
6	Mange
7	Quirrik
8	Yerg
9	Gnarok
10	Klix

SKAVEN EGOMANIACAL TITLES	
D10	**NAME**
1	Slayer of Man-things
2	the Most-Favoured
3	Lord of the Lash
4	Grand-Whiskers
5	Pox-Blessed
6	Blade-Tail
7	the Swift and Cunning
8	Almost-Loyal
9	the Great Opportunist
10	Stab-in-the-Back

ORIGIN	
1	**Suicide Mission** – Your clan's ruler has sent you on this mission thoroughly expecting you to fail.
2	**Realmstone Hunters** – Your warband is searching for realmstone deposits to power the death-dealing contraptions of the Skryre clans.
3	**Plague Seekers** – Your warband hunts for ingredients to brew one of the legendary Great Plagues on behalf of the Clans Pestilens.
4	**Killing Shadows** – Your warriors are talented assassins, hunting down those marked for death.
5	**To Mould Monsters** – At the command of your masters, your warband is looking for prime specimens with which to craft terrible monsters.
6	**Natural-born Schemers** – Your warriors are constantly looking for ways to undermine one another.

LEADER/FAVOURED WARRIOR BACKGROUND	
1	**Black Hunger** – This warrior's furious metabolism demands he constantly feed or otherwise perish.
2	**Warlock's Favourite** – This warrior has been 'rewarded' by the Skryre warlocks with new – and untested – inventions and weapons.
3	**The Withered Word** – This warrior's squeaking oratory inspires a limited form of courage in their minions.
4	**Shade of Murder** – No wall or gatehouse can stop this warrior from reaching their prey.
5	**It's Alive!** – The mutated rat-beasts raised by this warrior are truly horrific examples of their kind.
6	**Vicious Fighter** – This warrior is a surprisingly courageous fighter – for a skaven, at least.

SLAVES TO DARKNESS

Hellish champions of the Chaos Gods, the Slaves to Darkness fight in pursuit of immortality. As they slay their foes and honour the Ruinous Powers, these warriors receive infernal blessings, further fuelling their lust for conquest.

The tribes of the Slaves to Darkness represent the greater part of humanity found in the Mortal Realms. Their champions seek to walk the Path to Glory, the metaphysical road upon which a warrior's deeds are rewarded with Chaotic boons. Most coveted of these rewards is an eternity of war as a mighty Daemon Prince. The greatest overlords rule Hordes of thousands of warriors, but countless smaller warbands exist and seek glory of their own. Across the Bloodwind Spoil they battle for dominance, honouring the gods with each slaughtered enemy.

SLAVES TO DARKNESS FIRST NAMES	
D10	**NAME**
1	Engra
2	Kardoc
3	Hroth
4	Strykaar
5	Harahath
6	Arkorga
7	Ranlof
8	Malakh
9	Korag
10	Thoromus

SLAVES TO DARKNESS LAST NAMES	
D10	**NAME**
1	Varx
2	Blackrune
3	Shaargol
4	Deathsword
5	Kul
6	Ironsoul
7	Travos
8	Swordsson
9	Varkarian
10	Daemonblood

	ORIGIN
1	**The Path to Ruin** – Through acts of carnage, your warband has begun to attract the gaze of the gods.
2	**Lords of the Battlefield** – These warriors do not miss an opportunity to prove their prowess in battle.
3	**The Dark Arts** – Your warband serves the tribal shamans by seeking out arcane treasures and fonts of eldritch power.
4	**Spreaders of Corruption** – You and your warriors seek to spread the taint of Chaos far and wide.
5	**Host of Conquerors** – Your warband has fought among the conquering armies of the Everchosen himself.
6	**Godtouched** – Your warriors are deeply devoted to the worship of one particular aspect of Chaos.

	LEADER/FAVOURED WARRIOR BACKGROUND
1	**The Mark of Chaos** – This warrior has earned the mark of one of the Ruinous Powers.
2	**Infamous Warleader** – This warrior's diabolic charisma sees many would-be champions flock to their banner.
3	**Infernal Knowledge** – This warrior has fought for many years and has seen much of the dark power of Chaos.
4	**Touched by the Divine** – It is said that daemonic power courses through this warrior's veins.
5	**Brand of the Everchosen** – This warrior bears Archaon's own eight-pointed mark on their flesh or armour.
6	**Exalted** – Bloody omens suggest that this warrior is destined for greatness in the eyes of the gods.

CHAOS FATED QUESTS

Warriors fight for many reasons, be it the pursuit of treasure, lust for power or a simple love of war. Those who battle amidst the Bloodwind Spoil are no different, though each warlord's story is defined by their choices and character.

In this section you will find 4 special campaign quests known as **fated quests**. To use these quests, refer to page 63 of the Core Book.

AGENTS OF CHAOS

The fated quests in this book each have the **Chaos** runemark (☀). This means they can only be embarked upon by Chaos warbands (pg 4).

When embarking upon one of these fated quests, you can choose 1 Chaos faction runemark (pg 4) to apply to the fated quest.

The fated quests in this book use the territory rules opposite.

TERRAIN CARDS

The terrain cards for the fated quests in this book use scenery models from *Warcry: Catacombs*.

If you do not have the scenery models from *Warcry: Catacombs* but you do have scenery models from either a Ravaged Lands terrain set or the older *Warcry Starter Set*, the player controlling the Adversary warband can choose one of the terrain cards from that set to use instead.

CHAOS FATED QUEST TERRITORY RULES

Dominate Territory: *As the power of a warband grows, so too does the extent of the territory to which it can lay claim.*

You can spend 10 glory points to dominate a territory. Mark on your warband roster how many territories you dominate.

Dominating territory offers the following bonus:

For each territory dominated by your warband, increase the points you have available to spend on fighters when mustering your warband for a campaign battle by 50.

In addition, for each territory dominated by your warband, you can include 1 thrall in your warband when mustering for a campaign battle.

Thralls included in this manner are not added to your warband roster and cost points like any other fighter. Thralls can never gain destiny levels, bear artefacts or be chosen to become a favoured warrior.

HONOUR OR GLORY

Even the most noble champion may occasionally sully their soul in pursuit of glory, whilst a black-hearted rogue can reveal themselves to possess a shred of honour – albeit only if it benefits them to show it. In the corrupted lands of the Eightpoints it is a warrior's deeds alone that define them, and that chart the course of their destiny.

The campaign outcomes for fated quests differ from those in the Core Book. When you complete a fated quest, you have to make a choice between **Honour** or **Glory** before you claim your reward.

If you choose Glory, your reward will be an artefact of power. If you choose Honour, your reward will be an **exalted** command trait.

EXALTED COMMAND TRAITS

Exalted command traits represent qualities so strong they come to define a warrior for the rest of their life. The first time you receive an exalted command trait, this must be given to your leader, and it replaces any existing command trait that they might have.

Once your leader has been given an exalted command trait, any future exalted command traits received are discarded. Exalted command traits can never be given to a favoured warrior.

93

CRIMSON BOUNTY

FINAL CONVERGENCE
Hunter's Camp

SECOND CONVERGENCE
Plains of the Daemonroost

FIRST CONVERGENCE
Ancient Barrows

In Carngrad, every day is a battle to cling onto power. As is the case with all battles, inevitably there are losers. Gorthon Skraith, a former Talon of Carngrad, and his followers have recently been run out of the city following a sudden and violent coup by his rivals. However, these power-hungry revolutionaries made a mistake which could yet prove fatal – they did not succeed in slaying Skraith outright.

Now a bounty has been put on Skraith's head, and warriors from across the Bloodwind Spoil rush to collect it. His whereabouts are unknown, but doubtless he has a plan of his own in mind. Whether you wish to obtain the reward, impress a powerful patron or simply hear the deposed Talon scream, run him to the ground and resolve this matter with typical brutality.

D3	ARTEFACT OF POWER
1	**Staff of Dark Dreaming:** *Enemies struck by this writhing stave see the world through a strange haze of unreality, rendering them eminently vulnerable.* If an attack action made by the bearer that has a Range characteristic of 3 or less scores any critical hits, roll a dice. On a 4+, the target fighter cannot be picked to activate in that battle round.
2	**Fleshhunt Familiar:** *This skull once belonged to a skilled hunter. Now marked with unholy sigils, it whispers of enemies who seek the refuge of cover.* Enemy fighters cannot receive the benefit of cover when they are targeted by an attack action made by the bearer.
3	**Varanite Warblade:** *Those struck by this blade are afflicted with hideous transmutative growths.* If an attack action made by the bearer that has a Range characteristic of 3 or less scores any critical hits, halve the Move characteristic of the target fighter until the end of the battle round.

D3	COMMAND TRAIT
1	**Dread Favour:** *The watching gods of ruin have marked this champion for a dark destiny.* During the aftermath sequence, when rolling for destiny levels, this fighter gains a destiny level on a 5+.
2	**Dark Charisma:** *This champion wields their force of personality as a weapon, their words alone enough to fill their servants with fanatical zeal.* This fighter can use the 'Inspiring Presence' ability as a [double] instead of a [triple]. In addition, they can use this ability even if they do not have the **Leader** runemark (☼).
3	**Ruinous Duellist:** *Only the truly desperate, or truly foolish, would willingly enter a one-on-one confrontation with this superlative warrior.* While there is only 1 enemy fighter within 3" of this fighter, add 2 to the Attacks characteristic of attack actions made by this fighter that have a Range characteristic of 3 or less.

FIRST CONVERGENCE: THE COMPETITION

You are determined to be the one who claims the blood-price on Gorthon Skraith – and the gods have never frowned upon fighting a little dirty. Another warband seems to be following the same trail as you; they could infringe upon your ambitions if left unchecked. You will wait until they are defenceless and out of position before striking them down.

BATTLEPLAN
Terrain: See map.

Deployment: Draw a deployment card as normal.

Victory: No Mercy

Twist: The Aspirant player picks 1 twist card to be in play.

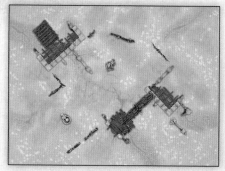

SECOND CONVERGENCE: PAYING A HOUSE CALL

Word has spread that Gorthon Skraith recently consulted with a hermit sorcerer dwelling in the beast-haunted region known as the Daemonroost. You should pay this sorcerer a visit of your own. Other bounty-hunting warbands have had a similar idea, and are currently battling their way through the monsters that stalk the Daemonroost. You must reach your goal before they do.

BATTLEPLAN
Terrain: See map.

Deployment: Draw a deployment card as normal.

Victory: The Gauntlet

The Aspirant warband is the defender.

Twist: Rampaging Beasts

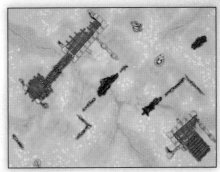

FINAL CONVERGENCE: END OF THE LINE

The sorcerer, under some duress, revealed that Skraith sought the location of an ancient network of temples and ruins nestled amongst the mountains; within, it is said, can be found potent treasures and mystical secrets that could ensure his return to power. You catch up with the former Talon and his last loyal warriors just as he heads into the ruins. Fight your way through Skraith's elite guards and ensure he goes no further.

BATTLEPLAN
Terrain: See map.

Deployment: Frontal Assault

The Aspirant warband uses the red deployment points.

Victory: Cut Off the Head

Twist: Eager for the Fight and No Holding Back

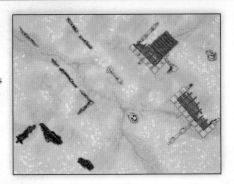

CAMPAIGN OUTCOME

If the Aspirant warband is the winner, they complete this campaign quest. Read the text below, and then choose either **Honour** or **Glory**.

You find Skraith shortly after entering one of the inner chambers of the temple, disarming the last few traps and rifling through the cobwebbed artefacts hidden within. The former Talon is unsurprised to see you. He would, after all, have been the first to send hired hunters after a vulnerable rival were his position reversed – such is life in the Bloodwind Spoil. Even so, the mortal champion no doubt desires to live. While he holds no grudge against you personally, he promises to make it a hard fight before you can lay him low. Such a claim is no doubt partially born from defiant hubris, for you outnumber him considerably. Still, his guards did not fall easily, and Skraith has enough strength remaining to present a challenge.

However, perhaps it need not come to that. Whatever the Talons of Carngrad have offered you, Skraith offers a reward just as valuable in return for staying your blade; namely, helping you to uncover the secrets of this temple-vault and claim the prize within. There are ancient magics here that, were you to harness them, could see your warband rise to new heights of glory. Skraith claims to already be most of the way there – and when weighed against the value of his life, he is willing to share in the reward. Still, a pact was made with the lords of Carngrad – Gorthon Skraith must die. Will you honour this arrangement, or assist Skraith in unlocking greater power?

HONOUR	**GLORY**
If you choose Honour, turn to page 102 to see the outcome and claim your reward.	If you choose Glory, turn to page 103 to see the outcome and claim your reward.

THE GRAND PLAGUE OF VETCH

FINAL CONVERGENCE
Bloody Streets

SECOND CONVERGENCE
Squatters' Haunt

FIRST CONVERGENCE
Loot Caravan

As the old saying goes, skaven society is a tyranny moderated by assassination. Each of the ratmen is forever seeking to increase their own power, at the cost of all their immediate rivals and betters. In order to disguise their conniving schemes, some skaven look to hire warbands from outside their own kind, or at least look for fellow ratmen with whom they cannot be immediately associated.

Your warband has recently been hired by the Plague Priest Vetch the Most-Pustulent to aid in his scheme to infect many of his rivals in the warrens of Under-Carngrad. The political machinations of the ratman are of little personal interest – but having him in your debt, or even just creating a little anarchy, might be worth due consideration.

D3	ARTEFACT OF POWER
1	**Rustblessed Blade:** *The merest scratch from this corroded dagger sees armour crumble and flake.* If an attack action made by the bearer that has a Range characteristic of 3 or less scores any critical hits, subtract 5 from target fighter's Toughness characteristic (to a minimum of 1) until the end of the battle round.
2	**Cowl of Living Night:** *One who wears this forbidding cowl seems to become a living shadow.* Subtract 1 from the Attacks characteristic (to a minimum of 1) of attack actions that target the bearer.
3	**Vial of Mysteries:** *You aren't entirely sure what this potion is made of, but something tells you it can offer great power to the worthy…* Roll a dice when a fighter is given this artefact. On a 1-3, add 5 to the Wounds characteristic of that fighter. On a 4+, add 1 to the Move characteristic of that fighter.

D3	COMMAND TRAIT
1	**A Nose for Trouble:** *This warrior seems to have a preternatural sense for imminent danger, and can react accordingly.* Subtract 1 (to a minimum of 1) from the damage points allocated to this fighter by each hit and critical hit from attack actions made by enemy fighters.
2	**Bolstered by Corruption:** *This champion is so redolent with dark energies that the poisons and maladies of the enemy can do nothing to weaken their defences.* Add 1 to the Toughness characteristic of this fighter. In addition, any rule that subtracts from a fighter's Toughness characteristic has no effect on this fighter.
3	**Insidious Schemer:** *This warrior's plans are as labyrinthine as they are effective.* If this fighter is included in your warband, you begin the battle with 1 additional wild dice.

FIRST CONVERGENCE: TAINTED LARDER

Vetch requires several highly specific ingredients to brew his most magnificent plague – daemon hearts, ogre brains, Harkraken livers and other things you have never even heard of. Fortunately, the Plague Priest believes that a loot caravan recently returned to Carngrad contains many of the items he requires. Prepare an ambush to strip the caravan's masters of their esoteric valuables.

BATTLEPLAN
Terrain: See map.

Deployment: Draw a deployment card as normal.

Victory: Defend the Find

The Aspirant warband is the attacker.

Twist: Draw a twist card as normal.

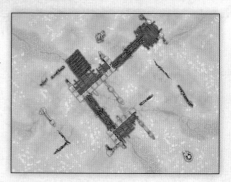

SECOND CONVERGENCE: WHAT'S YOURS IS MINE

Vetch is a cunning one, and knows that brewing his potent plague in the Screaming Delve beneath Carngrad would invite swift retribution from his fellow skaven. Instead, he intends to use your warriors to find an area of Carngrad in which to base his operation. You soon discover an appropriate site, but it is inhabited already by local thugs and squatter-warbands. Clear them out with extreme prejudice.

BATTLEPLAN
Terrain: See map.

Deployment: Draw a deployment card as normal.

Victory: Drawn and Quartered

Twist: Draw a twist card as normal

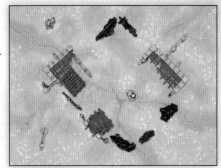

FINAL CONVERGENCE: POWER REBALANCED

You fully expected your dealings to come to the attention of Vetch's rivals eventually. In all honesty, you expected the Plague Priest himself to be the one to scheme for your death. However, the hired assassins that corner you in a dark alleyway seem to be in the employ of another skaven potentate – judging by the cruel-looking weapons they wield, at least. Either way, you must thwart this brazen attempt on your life.

BATTLEPLAN
Terrain: See map.

Deployment: Draw a deployment card as normal.

Victory: Assassinate

The Aspirant warband is the Defender.

Twist: Draw a twist card as normal.

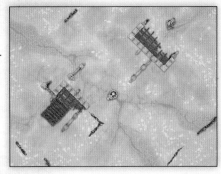

CAMPAIGN OUTCOME

If the Aspirant warband is the winner, they complete this campaign quest. Read the text below, and then choose either **Honour** or **Glory**.

As you slay the last assassin, mocking applause rings out from the shadows. A crooked snout emerges, festooned with tattered whiskers. It belongs to a white-furred creature clutching a gnarled staff, his skull crowned with twisting horns. The Grey Seer admits that he did not expect the assassins to slay you – which is almost certainly a lie – but now, he wishes to speak. The sorcerer has learnt of Vetch's plan, and is most displeased. He has plots of his own in motion amongst the clans of Under-Carngrad, all of which are now threatened by the Plague Priest's ambition. However, he believes there is a way to turn this potential disaster to mutual advantage – albeit not for Vetch.

From beneath his flea-bitten robes the Grey Seer produces a flask that glows with sinister light; within, he claims, are mystical ingredients that will pervert Vetch's plague. Those afflicted will enter a furious rage that will likely see the Plague Priest overwhelmed by a horde of rabid ratmen. All the Grey Seer asks is that you smuggle the ingredients into Vetch's great brew – do this, and you will be most handsomely rewarded. You could remain loyal to the Plague Priest, benefiting from his rise to power – or, renege on your already limited honour and increase your prestige amongst the Grey Seers. The choice is yours.

HONOUR
If you choose Honour, turn to page 102 to see the outcome and claim your reward.

GLORY
If you choose Glory, turn to page 103 to see the outcome and claim your reward.

FIT FOR A KING

SECOND CONVERGENCE
Unfortunate Allies

FINAL CONVERGENCE
Forge of the Bullfather

FIRST CONVERGENCE
Aelven Corpses

The denizens of the Eightpoints are far more likely to be concerned with desecration than creation, but this is not a universal truth. The warrior-smiths of the Iron Golems and Skullgrinders of the Blood God are perhaps the most famed examples of these malevolent artisans, but there are other binders of steel and souls to be discovered and treated with in this land if one knows where to search.

To the east of Lost Velorum stands a lonely forge tower; it is said that the daemon-touched master of this place will craft a mighty weapon for any who brings him a sufficiently worthy offering. Armed with such an artefact, you know you would destroy your rivals and soon ascend to new heights of power. You will do whatever it takes to acquire it.

D3	ARTEFACT OF POWER
1	**Cuirass of the Slaughtering Brute:** *The deadly spikes and tusks that protrude from this plate turn the wearer's sheer momentum into a weapon.* Each time the bearer finishes a move action, visible enemy fighters within 1" of them suffer impact damage.
2	**Oblivion Mantle:** *So steeped in unholy energies is this armour that it can hold death itself at bay.* Once per battle, the first time the bearer is taken down by an attack action, they are not taken down. Instead, you can remove D6 damage points allocated to them, and any damage points that remain to be allocated from that attack action are discarded.
3	**Daemonic Familiar:** *This infernal imp attacks its master's foes with commendable conviction.* Each time the bearer finishes an attack action, visible enemy fighters within 1" of them suffer impact damage.

D3	COMMAND TRAIT
1	**Carnage Eternal:** *Bloodshed alone is enough to satisfy this deadly warrior.* Each time this fighter takes down an enemy fighter, you can remove D3 damage points allocated to this fighter.
2	**Master of Dark Rituals:** *The profane acts performed by this champion ensure that the power of Chaos clings to them like an unholy shroud.* Each time this fighter takes down an enemy fighter, you gain 1 additional wild dice that can be used in the hero phase of the next battle round.
3	**Artisan of Obliteration:** *This warrior is a talented bladesmith in their own right, modifying their weapons to render them more deadly still.* Add 1 to the damage points allocated to enemy fighters by each hit and critical hit from attack actions made by this fighter that have a Range characteristic of 3 or less.

FIRST CONVERGENCE: ARCHAON'S GIFT

It is said that the smith-master asks for two things in return for his service: the first is varanite, the warping molten realmstone of the Eightpoints. Most varanite veins run far below the surface, but you have chanced upon the remains of an aelven party carrying sealed containers of the realmstone. You must not waste this opportunity, for other warbands have been drawn to the kill, and seek to seize the precious resource for themselves.

BATTLEPLAN
Terrain: See map.

Deployment: Draw a deployment card as normal.

Victory: Realmstone Hunt

Twist: Draw a twist card as normal.

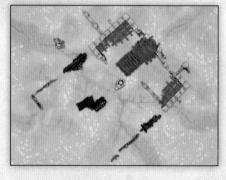

SECOND CONVERGENCE: YOU STAB MY BACK

With the varanite in your possession, you must acquire the second offering. This one, however, may prove more taxing. The daemon-smith demands the heart of an ally, claimed in combat. A warband you have fought beside in the past is passing through the area after a successful raid. Their leader will no doubt fight furiously in response to this betrayal. Strike them down regardless.

BATTLEPLAN
Terrain: See map.

Deployment: Draw a deployment card as normal.

Victory: Assassinate

The Aspirant warband is the attacker.

Twist: Bitter Rivals

FINAL CONVERGENCE: A RED PRICE

With the two offerings in your possession, you make your way into the mountains in search of the daemonic forge. It is not long before you spot thick clouds of ash belching into the sky, twisted smoke-stacks spearing the horizon. As you approach the forge-complex, you find the gates guarded by a band of watchmen. Speaking in unnerving synchronicity, they decree that only the worthy may stand before their master. Teach these upstart fools a lesson.

BATTLEPLAN
Terrain: See map.

Deployment:
Show of Strength

The Aspirant warband uses the red deployment points.

Victory: No Mercy

Twist: Battle of Wits and Foreboding Location

CAMPAIGN OUTCOME

If the Aspirant warband is the winner, they complete this campaign quest. Read the text below, and then choose either **Honour** or **Glory**.

Before you and the guards can finish tearing one another apart an echoing, grinding sound rings out. You restrain your urge to fall on your hesitating enemies as the doors to the forge swing open; as they do so, the guards disappear into clouds of flaking ash. It seems the defences of this place were more esoteric than you had anticipated. Collecting yourself, you beckon your warband to follow you inside. Navigating between vats of bubbling blood and screeching furnaces, you ascend the iron stairs of the forge until you stand in the sweltering chambers of its master.

The duardin who rules this place is clearly no longer entirely mortal; great tusks emerge from his lower jaw, while his eyes are aglow with infernal light. Ash spills from his mouth as he speaks, flickering flame-daemons sparking into being in the air around him. Standing before a great anvil-altar crowned with the image of a snorting bull, the duardin beckons you to present your tribute. He appraises your offerings carefully, but at last – to your slight relief – accepts them both. In return, he offers you a difficult choice. Do you wish for dominion? To become a great ruler and expand your conquests further across the Bloodwind Spoil? Or is it greater might in battle that you desire – to strike down all who dare stand before you and earn the favour of the gods through glorious carnage?

HONOUR	**GLORY**
If you choose Honour, turn to page 102 to see the outcome and claim your reward.	If you choose Glory, turn to page 103 to see the outcome and claim your reward.

BENEATH SHADOWED BOUGHS

First Convergence
Witchlight Debris

Final Convergence
Heart of the Shadows

Second Convergence
Ruins of Nar'az Drom

Half-remembered legend tells that even in the lost Age of Myth, something was amiss within the Black Knife forest. Insular druidic covens met amongst the twisted trees, performing disturbing rites at the behest of unseen nature gods. Although the Black Knife forest is long gone, and even the city that was built atop its levelled ground now lies in ruin, an unsettling aura still clings to this lonely place.

But you fear no gheist or spectre – that is what you tell yourself, at least. Drawn to the ruins that lie atop the heart of the old forest by the whispers in your mind – surely the voices of the gods – it feels as if glory is but a hair's breadth away. But the voices are insistent – you must reach your destination swiftly, for rival warbands have also been drawn here in pursuit of lost secrets.

D3	ARTEFACT OF POWER
1	**Wyldbark Crown:** *The power of this oaken crown bestows the wearer's allies with the untrammelled might of the wild.* Add 1 to the Strength characteristic of attack actions that have a Range characteristic of 3 or less made by friendly fighters while they are within 9" of the bearer.
2	**Souleater Venom:** *The venom of souleater spiders needs only the merest of scratches to do its work.* Each time an attack action made by the bearer that has a Range characteristic of 3 or less scores any critical hits, subtract 1 from the Attacks characteristic (to a minimum of 1) of attack actions made by the target fighter until the end of the battle.
3	**Raptoryx-feather Charm:** *A portion of a Raptoryx's boundless ferocity is passed on to those who wear these gore-slicked feathers.* Add 1 to the Move characteristic of the bearer.

D3	COMMAND TRAIT
1	**Lord of Dominion:** *This warrior revels in exerting their strength and power over those they deem to be lesser beings.* The Strength characteristic of attack actions made by this fighter count as being higher than the target's Toughness characteristic unless the target has the **Leader** runemark (☼) or **Gargantuan** runemark (🐾).
2	**Unnatural Vitality:** *Like a gnarled and twisted oak that will not fall, this champion stands inviolate against the enemy's pathetic blows.* Add 5 to the Wounds characteristic of this fighter.
3	**Hack and Slash:** *Eventually, all warriors fall like trees. This champion considers themselves to be the lumberjack.* Add 1 to the Attacks characteristic of attack actions made by this fighter that have a Range characteristic of 3 or less.

FIRST CONVERGENCE: WHISPERS AND WITCH-LIGHTS

For days you have trekked the twisting paths of the ruins, occasionally encountering other warbands before finding yourself isolated once more. In the shadows of ancient grandeur you witness wisps of fey light dancing in the dark, beckoning you onwards. Others have spotted them, believing themselves to be chosen. Pursue the wisps and let them lead you towards your destiny.

BATTLEPLAN
Terrain: See map.

Deployment: Draw a deployment card as normal.

Victory: Hunt for Glory

Twist: Dusk

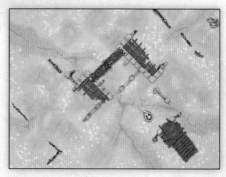

SECOND CONVERGENCE: NAR'AZ DROM

An eerie silence has descended upon the ruins; even the wind seems cowed by the stillness. Eventually, you spot a tall structure rising up ahead. You realise you have chanced upon the storied hall of Nar'az Drom, where it is said the wealthy lords of this forgotten city once held court. Perhaps here you can find your promised riches, though first you must slay those who now squat amidst the ruins.

BATTLEPLAN

Terrain: See map.

Deployment: Draw a deployment card as normal.

Victory: Seize Territory

The Aspirant warband is the attacker.

Twist: Eerie Silence

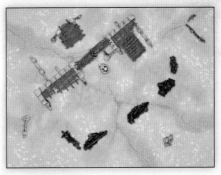

FINAL CONVERGENCE: GODS OF OUR FATHERS

Nar'az Drom lies empty of treasure. You are beginning to wonder if it really is the gods that guide you, or some other sinister force. At last you reach a square that must once have been the forest's heart. Vines choke the tumbled stone, and you could swear you are being watched from the shadows. Another warband is already here, just as lost as you. As your eyes lock, you are hit with realisation – only one warband will be allowed to walk away.

BATTLEPLAN

Terrain: See map.

Deployment: Frontal Assault

Victory: Cut off the Head

Twist: No Holding Back

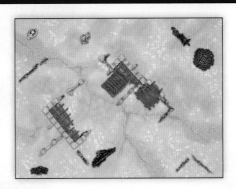

CAMPAIGN OUTCOME

If the Aspirant warband is the winner, they complete this campaign quest. Read the text below, and then choose either **Honour** or **Glory**.

Ducking and weaving beneath the desperate blows of your adversaries, you have time to consider the events that led you here. Perhaps you should have known that there would be some trick afoot – or maybe you did expect as much, and simply wished to investigate the whispers that coursed through your mind. Either way, it is irrelevant now. Whatever atavistic beings linger here have played you false; rather than golden treasure or mind-shattering secrets, this central square has revealed nothing more than another killing ground on which to satisfy their bloody thirsts. To allow you to leave, they demand one final offering of blood. Many would respond to such deceit with violence, turning upon the spirits once these latest enemies have been dealt with. Such would almost be the kinder option, preventing any in the future from falling to the old forest's sibilant lures.

And yet, as you strike down the last of your foes, you can sense the shadows shuddering in anticipation. Rarely have the spirits been offered such a magnificent bounty upon which to feast. Stay your hand and leave them to gorge themselves upon the essences of those who proved unworthy, and perhaps you will be rewarded. Blood dripping from your blade, you listen as your warband slays the few remaining enemies. A decision looms – will you punish the darkling entities for their defiance and see them consumed in the fires of your wrath, or will you risk everything and accept a boon from the lords of Black Knife?

HONOUR

If you choose Honour, turn to page 102 to see the outcome and claim your reward.

GLORY

If you choose Glory, turn to page 103 to see the outcome and claim your reward.

SPOILS OF VICTORY

Through battle and bloodshed, you and your warband have emerged triumphant. Across the Bloodwind Spoil lie the broken remains of your foes, their ambition no match for your cunning and skill-at-arms. Whether you will cleave to an honourable path, or risk damning yourself in pursuit of greater glory, is up to you to decide…

On these pages you will find conclusions for each of the narrative campaign quests provided in this book. If you chose the path to Honour, you will find your reward on this page. If you chose the path to Glory, your reward awaits on the page opposite.

HONOUR

CRIMSON BOUNTY – A PACT MAINTAINED

Skraith curses you for a witless fool as you draw your blades, muttering an oath to the Dark Gods. The battle that follows is ferocious, for the former Talon is a cornered animal now fighting for his life. Still, you prove the superior warrior. As Skraith's blood spatters across the walls, you take his head as proof of your victory. Let it be known that all those you consider your prey live only on borrowed time.

EXALTED COMMAND TRAIT
Terminal Blow: *This warrior is incredibly thorough when it comes to finishing off their foes.*

Add 5 to the damage points allocated by each critical hit from attack actions made by this fighter that have a Range characteristic of 3 or less.

THE GRAND PLAGUE OF VETCH – WRACK AND RUIN

For now, maintaining your pact with Vetch suits your goals. The Grey Seer hisses a promise of vengeance as he scampers back into the shadows; you warn the Plague Priest of the attempted meddling, keeping a close watch as the potent pox is brewed. As Vetch's disciples begin transporting vials of the resulting concoction throughout the warrens, you revel in your success. No doubt the Clans Pestilens will look favourably upon you now.

EXALTED COMMAND TRAIT
Corruptor's Gifts: *The plague lords of the Clans Pestilens have taught this champion a clawful of valuable secrets concerning contagion and disease.*

Once per battle, this fighter can use this command trait as an action. If they do so, pick a visible enemy fighter within 9" of this fighter. Allocate 2D6 damage points to that fighter.

FIT FOR A KING – INFERNUS REX

You crave rulership, to dominate the weak and establish yourself as a mighty ruler. In response, the daemon-smith crafts a crown that crackles with an otherworldly light. As soon as you place it upon your brow, it fuses hideously to your flesh – the pain is intense, but brief. With this power, the daemon-smith claims, your commands will be obeyed without fear or complaint. Truly, it is a worthy prize for a conqueror such as yourself.

EXALTED COMMAND TRAIT
Overlord of Ruin: *This warrior is a conqueror born, and with each new land they claim, their power and favour only seem to increase.*

At the start of each battle round, before the hero phase begins, roll a number of dice equal to number of territories this fighter's warband dominates. For each 6, you gain 1 wild dice.

BENEATH SHADOWED BOUGHS – ASHES TO ASHES

There is no glory to be won here, only an endless cycle of death to feed the ravenous entities' hunger. Such deception must be punished. You can almost hear the screaming of the corrupted nature-spirits as your warriors begin setting about the overgrown ruins with flaming torches. As the crackle of flames intensifies, you smile. Such is the price of playing you false.

EXALTED COMMAND TRAIT
Fearsome Destroyer: *Nothing is allowed to stand between this warrior and victory – certainly not their weakling foes.*

Once per battle, this fighter can use this command trait to make a bonus move action or a bonus attack action.

CRIMSON BOUNTY – RENEGOTIATION

Skraith has a point: you have no real stake in the Talons' squabbles. If you can benefit through this temporary alliance, all the better. With the knowledge Skraith received from the sorcerer you are able to penetrate deeper into the ruins, finally arriving at an ancient treasure vault. Breaching its wards, you find within a shield wrought in the image of a snarling daemon-hound. Waves of dread emanate from it, sending a brief shiver through you. In return for sparing him, Skraith insists that you take it – not that he could stop you, anyway.

ARTEFACT OF POWER
Daemonmaw Shield: *The black-gem eyes of this shield seem to watch you wherever you go. Those fixed by its hideous gaze are paralysed by a wave of other-worldly dread.*

Once per battle, the bearer can use this artefact as a bonus action. If they do so, pick 1 visible enemy fighter within 9" of them and roll a dice. On a 2+, that fighter cannot make move actions or disengage actions until the end of the battle round.

THE GRAND PLAGUE OF VETCH – RECIPE FOR DISASTER

It is not difficult to introduce the rogue element to Vetch's brew; a bribe here, an opportune assassination there, and you have everything in place. Even as Vetch croons over his triumph, the mystic contamination desired by the Grey Seer subtly spreads throughout the pox. As you watch the plague-broth being collected for distribution throughout Under-Carngrad – its true nature unknown, for now – you smile and pat the cruel dagger strapped tight to your waist, a token of appreciation from the order of Grey Seers.

ARTEFACT OF POWER
The Shadowfang: *Thirteen strange symbols glow across the hilt of this dagger. Its wielder is able to cut holes in reality itself, emerging seemingly from nowhere to strike their prey.*

Once per battle, this fighter can use this artefact as a bonus action. If they do so, roll a dice. Then, you can remove the fighter from the battlefield and immediately set them up anywhere on the battlefield more than a number of inches of any enemy fighters equal to the roll.

FIT FOR A KING – SLAUGHTERER'S DAWN

To kill, to slaughter, to reave life and strike down your foes – these are the things that grant you purpose. Slaughter, and slaughter alone, won you the items which you now offer in tribute. In return for them, the daemon-smith agrees to forge you a mighty blade redolent with dark power; only the truly worthy may wield it without succumbing to its power, he warns, but surely that will be no problem for you. The ruin it can work on flesh and even soul is well worth it.

ARTEFACT OF POWER
Blade of the Stonefire Curse: *This blade blazes with dark fire yet never seems to burn you. Any struck by it will be lashed with unclean flames even as they find their body petrifying to unfeeling stone.*

Subtract 2 from the damage points allocated by each hit and critical hit (to a minimum of 1) from attack actions that target the bearer.

BENEATH SHADOWED BOUGHS – SACRAMENT OF BLOOD

As the last of your foes chokes on their own gore, resolution crystallises within you. Ancient things dwell here, and their hunger is insatiable. You do not appreciate the deception, but still you step back, letting the thirsting spirits have their due. Before your eyes the blood and bodies of the slain sink into the earth, devoured in their entirety. In their place rises a simple dagger, its wooden hilt carved with ancient sigils. The spirits are pleased with your offering, and will let you walk free from their domain – this time…

ARTEFACT OF POWER
Cursed Athame: *Across the centuries, thousands have died screaming beneath this simple dagger's edge. The blade hungers constantly for blood, strengthening they that feed it in turn.*

Each time the bearer takes down an enemy fighter, you can remove D6 damage points allocated to the bearer.

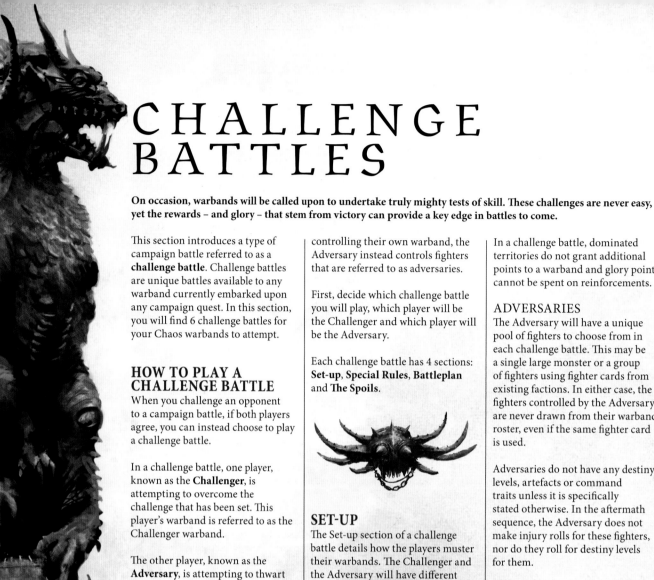

CHALLENGE BATTLES

On occasion, warbands will be called upon to undertake truly mighty tests of skill. These challenges are never easy, yet the rewards – and glory – that stem from victory can provide a key edge in battles to come.

This section introduces a type of campaign battle referred to as a **challenge battle**. Challenge battles are unique battles available to any warband currently embarked upon any campaign quest. In this section, you will find 6 challenge battles for your Chaos warbands to attempt.

HOW TO PLAY A CHALLENGE BATTLE

When you challenge an opponent to a campaign battle, if both players agree, you can instead choose to play a challenge battle.

In a challenge battle, one player, known as the **Challenger**, is attempting to overcome the challenge that has been set. This player's warband is referred to as the Challenger warband.

The other player, known as the **Adversary**, is attempting to thwart the Challenger. Rather than controlling their own warband, the Adversary instead controls fighters that are referred to as adversaries.

First, decide which challenge battle you will play, which player will be the Challenger and which player will be the Adversary.

Each challenge battle has 4 sections: **Set-up**, **Special Rules**, **Battleplan** and **The Spoils**.

SET-UP

The Set-up section of a challenge battle details how the players muster their warbands. The Challenger and the Adversary will have different rules they must follow.

In a challenge battle, dominated territories do not grant additional points to a warband and glory points cannot be spent on reinforcements.

ADVERSARIES

The Adversary will have a unique pool of fighters to choose from in each challenge battle. This may be a single large monster or a group of fighters using fighter cards from existing factions. In either case, the fighters controlled by the Adversary are never drawn from their warband roster, even if the same fighter card is used.

Adversaries do not have any destiny levels, artefacts or command traits unless it is specifically stated otherwise. In the aftermath sequence, the Adversary does not make injury rolls for these fighters, nor do they roll for destiny levels for them.

THE PREREQUISITE AND THE STAKE

Every challenge battle has a **prerequisite** and a **stake**. The prerequisite is the required number of dominated territories the Challenger warband must have. If the Challenger warband does not meet the prerequisite, the challenge battle cannot be played.

If the Challenger warband loses the challenge battle, they immediately lose a number of dominated territories equal to the stake. This represents the repercussions that the warband faces in the wake of their failure and the time they must spend recuperating their resources.

SPECIAL RULES

Challenge battles may have 1 or more **special rules**. These can be rules that apply to some or all fighters – akin to twists – or rules that alter the core rules for generating a battle.

BATTLEPLAN

The Battleplan section of each challenge battle explains how to generate the battleplan.

THE SPOILS

Each challenge battle has 1 or more **spoils**. If the Challenger warband wins the challenge battle, they receive 1 of the spoils of that challenge battle. In some cases, they may receive bonus spoils for completing a specific task.

TREASURE HOARD

One of the spoils of each challenge battle is the treasure hoard. If the Challenger picks this reward, they can make up to 3 additional search rolls on the lesser artefacts table (Core Book, pg 68-69) during the aftermath sequence of the battle.

ARTEFACTS OF POWER

Some spoils grant an artefact of power to be given to one of the fighters in the Challenger warband. An artefact of power can only be given to a fighter if no other fighters in the same warband bear the same artefact of power.

MONSTERS

Some spoils will let you add the monster adversary to your warband roster. If you choose such a reward, use the rules on pages 8-10.

THE AFTERMATH SEQUENCE

After each challenge battle, resolve the aftermath sequence (Core Book, pg 66-70) with the following amendments:

- Players do not receive glory points for playing a challenge battle.

- Injury rolls and destiny rolls are not made for adversaries.

- Neither player advances on their campaign progress tracker.

Note that both players can make 1 search roll on the lesser artefacts table as normal. When the Adversary does so, they must pick a fighter from one of their warbands that is embarked on a campaign quest to receive the lesser artefact.

PLAYING AGAIN

You can play through the same challenge battle as many times as you wish, even if you have already achieved victory. Note that certain spoils, such as artefacts of power, are limited to 1 per warband roster.

The Narrative of Challenge Battles

Challenge battles allow players to explore the Eightpoints in more ways than ever before. Your warband might decide to hunt down a Chimera in its lair and, if successful, subjugate it or sell its most valuable parts in the local barter pits. In other challenge battles they might match themselves against an ancient, skeletal champion of the gods, or attempt to harvest potent varanite while fighting off hordes of Chaos Spawn.

These battles offer their own unique challenge and are suitable for up-and-coming warbands as well as those that have completed a campaign quest and are yet to embark on a new one. For such warbands, challenge battles offer a set of difficult trials to overcome and a checklist of achievements to complete.

If you are looking to add a monster to your warband through a challenge battle, it is expected that you will first collect and paint the model yourself before challenging a friend. You then get the chance to tame the wild monster and later add it to your warband roster, while your opponent gets the chance to run amok through your warband with a very dangerous beast!

Many of these challenge battles are designed to be very difficult for the Challenger, and completing all of them is something to boast about! It will require all your tactical cunning – and often an abundance of artefacts of power and destiny levels – to emerge victorious.

Good luck, and may the gods be on your side!

THE VARANITE HARVEST

Of the many deadly prizes to be found in the Bloodwind Spoil, varanite – also known as bloodrock, octarite and Archaon's Gift – is amongst the most infamous. This volatile realmstone seethes with the power of mutation, and even the merest contact with it can twist the body into hideous new form. Though it is undeniably perilous, it is highly sort after by certain champions, particularly arcane weaponsmiths and the Master Moulders of the skaven.

You have been hired by an interested party to obtain a haul of varanite, and granted several nullstone canisters to transport the molten realmstone. There is, however, a problem. Traveling to the deep caves of Varanthax's Maw, you find them infested with mewling Chaos Spawn – no doubt those who fell victim to the varanite's power. You must fight through the Spawn and other beasts that lurk within, collecting the varanite before you are overwhelmed.

SET-UP

Prerequisite: 2 dominated territories

Stake: 1 dominated territory

THE WARBANDS

The Challenger and the Adversary player each muster a warband as described in the core rules (Core Book, pg 36), with the following amendments:

1. The Challenger must muster a Chaos warband, and all fighters in the warband must be chosen from the Challenger's warband roster.

2. All fighters in the Adversary player's warband must have the **Chaotic Beasts** faction runemark (🕸) and the **Thrall** runemark (☿).

3. The Adversary player's warband does not need to include a leader.

4. The combined points value of the fighters in each warband cannot exceed 1,250.

BATTLEPLAN

Terrain: See map.

Deployment: Into the Breach

The Challenger's warband uses the blue deployment points.

Victory: Cursed Relics

Twist: Rumoured Riches

SPECIAL RULES

Battle Groups: The Challenger warband must be split into battle groups as normal.

The Adversary player's warband is split into 2 battle groups: the Dagger and the Shield. Neither battle group can have more than 1 additional fighter than the other.

The Swarm Descends: Each time a fighter in the Adversary player's warband is taken down, an identical fighter is added to that warband and placed in reserve. In the reserve phase of the next battle round, that fighter can be set up as a reserve fighter (*Warcry: Catacombs*, pg 27).

Hideous Mutation: If the Challenger warband is embarked on a campaign in champion mode (see the *Tome of Champions 2019*), each time a fighter from the Challenger's warband that does not have the **Leader** runemark (☼) is taken down due to the 'Cursed Relics' victory condition, roll a dice before the fighter is removed. On a 1, that fighter has mutated into a hideous Chaos Spawn! The fighter is slain (as if they had rolled the 'Slain' result on the Critical Injuries table), and 1 Chaos Spawn is added to the Adversary player's warband. The Adversary player sets up the Chaos Spawn within 1" of the slain fighter, who is then removed.

THE SPOILS

If the Challenger wins the battle, they can choose 1 of the following spoils:

Treasure Hoard: See page 105.

Artefact of Power: The Challenger can give 1 fighter in their warband the following artefact of power:

Axe of Unmaking: *Blessed with the power of rampant mutation, this bizarre axe hungrily devours steel, flesh and bone with equal relish.*

Roll a dice each time an enemy fighter is taken down by an attack action made by the bearer that has a Range characteristic of 3 or less. On a 6, the bearer can immediately make a bonus move action or a bonus attack action.

FURY OF THE WILD

All manner of terrible beasts can be found in the Eightpoints, stalking the warped wilds and preying upon isolated warbands. Some, such as Chimeras, Ghorgons and mutant gargants can be found all across the Mortal Realms; others are one-of-a-kind horrors that could only take shape in the heart of ruin. All are deadly propositions in a fight, for they take a malicious delight in savaging and slaughtering their hapless prey.

You have heard rumour of such a monster rampaging through the wilds surrounding Carngrad; perhaps you wish to slay it, carving it up for raw materials, or alternatively break its spirit and force it into your service. Either way you soon track the beast to its lair. The ground is thick and swampy, sweltering with an unnatural heat, but you are undaunted. Though the creature will fight fiercely on its home territory, you will not be denied.

SET-UP

Prerequisite: 2 dominated territories

Stake: 1 dominated territory

THE ADVERSARIES
The Adversary player musters a warband that consists of 1 fighter with the **Gargantuan** runemark (🝊).

THE CHALLENGER WARBAND
The Challenger musters a warband as described in the core rules (Core Book, pg 36), with the following amendments:

1. The Challenger must muster a Chaos warband, and all fighters in the warband must be chosen from the Challenger's warband roster.

2. The combined points value of the fighters in the warband cannot exceed 3 times the points value of the Adversary player's warband.

SPECIAL RULES

Battle Groups: The Challenger warband must be split into battle groups as normal. The adversary is not in any battle group.

The Hunt: Do not draw a terrain card, deployment card or twist card as normal. Instead, use the following rules:

Draw 3 terrain cards and place them face down. The players then roll off. If the Adversary player wins the roll-off, no cards are revealed. If the players tie, 1 card chosen by the Challenger player is revealed. If the Adversary player loses the roll-off, all the cards are revealed. The Challenger then picks 1 of the 3 terrain cards to be in play for the battle.

Repeat this process for the deployment card. Repeat this process for the twist card, but before drawing the 3 cards remove all twist cards with the **Wild Creatures** runemark (🝋) and all those with the **Fate** runemark (🜚).

Deployment: The Challenger sets up all their battle groups first. The Adversary player then picks 1 of their deployment points and sets up the adversary as normal.

BATTLEPLAN

Terrain: See 'The Hunt' in the Special Rules box.

Deployment: See 'The Hunt' in the Special Rules box.

Victory: A player wins the battle as soon as every fighter in their opponent's warband is taken down.

Twist: See 'The Hunt' in the Special Rules box.

THE SPOILS

If the Challenger wins the battle, they can choose 1 of the following spoils:

Treasure Hoard: See page 105.

Monster: The monster adversary can be added to the Challenger's warband roster (pg 8-10).

THE EVERCHOSEN'S REGARDS

Sigmar is an arrogant fool. The God-King claims to protect his people, but was it not Sigmar who retreated during the Age of Chaos and hid himself in Azyr? Is it not Sigmar who, even now, sends his lightning-revenants to fight on his behalf? Any chance to humble these warriors must be seized, for a blow struck against them is a blow struck against hated Sigmar also.

You have run down a band of Stormcast Eternals commanded by some preening champion, harrying them to the ruins of a Sigmarite temple. It is here that the enemy makes their stand, and here you will slaughter the Stormcasts on the steps of their own altars. Each of them is a mighty hero worthy of caution, but you have an edge of your own – a colossal beast of the wastes, howling for hallowed blood. The gods surely watch this battle of faith with interest – you must not fail in their eyes.

SET-UP

Prerequisite: 4 dominated territories

Stake: 1 dominated territory

THE WARBANDS
The Challenger and the Adversary player each muster a warband as described in the core rules (Core Book, pg 36), with the following amendments:

1. The Challenger must muster a Chaos warband, and all fighters in the Challenger's warband must be chosen from the Challenger's warband roster. In addition, if the Challenger does not have a fighter with the **Gargantuan** runemark (🔱) on their warband roster, they can add 1 fighter with the **Gargantuan** runemark (🔱) to their warband for this battle.

2. All fighters in the Adversary player's warband must have 1 of the following faction runemarks: **Stormcast Eternals Warrior Chamber** (🔱), **Stormcast Eternals Vanguard Auxiliary Chamber** (⚡) or **Stormcast Eternals Sacrosanct Chamber** (⚡).

3. The combined points value of the fighters in each warband cannot exceed 1,500.

SPECIAL RULES

The Sigmarite Temple: After terrain has been set up, the Adversary player places a scenery model on the battlefield to represent the temple's statue of Sigmar.

During the battle, the statue of Sigmar can be targeted by attack actions and abilities used by fighters in the Challenger's warband. The statue of Sigmar has a Toughness characteristic of 10 and a Wounds characteristic of 50. Once 50 damage points have been allocated to the statue of Sigmar, it is desecrated.

Favour of the Gods: The Challenger rolls a dice each time an adversary is taken down. On a 3+, they can pick a fighter in their warband to receive a boon. The type of boon corresponds to the roll, as shown below:

3　**Boon of Nurgle:** You can remove up to D3 damage points allocated to that fighter.

4　**Boon of Tzeentch:** That fighter can immediately make a bonus disengage action.

5　**Boon of Khorne:** That fighter can immediately make a bonus attack action.

6　**Boon of Slaanesh:** That fighter can immediately make a bonus move action.

BATTLEPLAN

Terrain: The Adversary player picks the terrain card.

Deployment: Defiant Stand

The Challenger's warband uses the red deployment points.

Victory: If at the end of a battle round the statue of Sigmar (see the Special Rules box) is desecrated, the Challenger wins the battle.

Otherwise, a player wins the battle as soon as every fighter in their opponent's warband is taken down.

Twist: Azyrite Lightning Storm

The 'Lightning Strike' ability has a value of 6 when used by a fighter in the Adversary player's warband.

THE SPOILS

If the Challenger wins the battle, they can choose 1 of the following spoils:

Treasure Hoard: See page 105.

Artefact of Power: The Challenger can give 1 fighter in their warband the following artefact of power:

Desecrated Meteoric Mail: *One of many abandoned relics within the temple, this suit of meteoric armour has been thoroughly profaned by your efforts. No doubt it will incense Azyrites even as it wards you from their blows.*

Subtract 1 from the damage points allocated by each hit and critical hit from attack actions that target the bearer.

BLADES IN THE DARKNESS

Your legend has spread far and wide across the Bloodwind Spoil. It is perhaps inevitable then that there are those who would seek to bring that legend to a terminal end. Word has reached you that shadowy agents under the command of the so-called High Oracle of Khaine, Morathi, have been dispatched to kill you. Rather than succumb to panic, however, you have decided to use this as a chance to prove your supremacy once more.

Over several days you have established and maintained a defensible position; if these Khainites wish to slay you, they will have to dare this most formidable of gauntlets. On a grim, moonless night the cloaked aelven assassins slip through the darkness, cruel blades held ready. You must prevent them from claiming your head, in so doing proving your defiance of the craven God-King and further cementing your dark renown.

SET-UP

Prerequisite: 2 dominated territories

Stake: 1 dominated territory

THE WARBANDS

The Challenger and the Adversary player each muster a warband as described in the core rules (Core Book, pg 36), with the following amendments:

1. The Challenger must muster a Chaos warband, and all fighters in the Challenger's warband must be chosen from the Challenger's warband roster.

2. All fighters in the Adversary player's warband must have the **Khainite Shadowstalkers** faction runemark (⟨⋈⟩).

3. The combined points value of the fighters in each warband cannot exceed 1,250.

SPECIAL RULES

Hidden Killers: Fighters in the Adversary player's warband are not split into battle groups. In addition, when setting up the battle, the Adversary does not set up any fighters from their warband on the battlefield. Instead, they set up 18 counters, 6 for each battle group, on the battlefield as if they were fighters. For the counters, we recommend using spare 25mm bases.

During the battle, the counters are treated as fighters in the Adversary player's warband and can make move actions with a Move characteristic of 6".

During the battle, the counters can be revealed by a number of means. When a counter is revealed, it is replaced by any fighter from the Adversary player's warband that has not yet been set up on the battlefield.

A counter is revealed as follows:

- If the counter is targeted by an ability or attack action.

- If the counter is within 6" of an enemy fighter at the end of any action.

- If the Adversary player reveals the counter, which they can do at any point during its activation.

Once all fighters from the Adversary player's warband have been set up, all remaining counters are removed from the battlefield.

BATTLEPLAN

Terrain: Draw 3 terrain cards; the Challenger player picks 1 of them to be in play.

Deployment: Defiant Stand

The Challenger uses the blue deployment points.

Victory: Assassinate

The Challenger is the defender

Twist: Dead of Night

THE SPOILS

If the Challenger wins the battle, they can choose 1 of the following spoils:

Treasure Hoard: See page 105.

Artefact of Power: The Challenger can give 1 fighter in their warband the following artefact of power:

Ulguan Duskbauble: *All that remains of your would-be assassins is this strange trinket. The air around it shimmers with a pall of shadow and half-glimpsed illusions that confound and distract.*

Subtract 1 from the Attacks characteristic (to a minimum of 1) of attack actions that target the bearer.

AN IRREFUTABLE CHALLENGE

Nagash's gaze has long been drawn to the Eightpoints. The Great Necromancer is a megalomaniac beyond compare, and to conquer the stronghold of the Everchosen would send a powerful message. Waves of Shyishan energies blight the lands, setting the slaughtered dead stirring. Even the fallen champions of the gods are not safe from Nagash's will.

Recently, word has spread of an ancient lord who has risen from the grave and now lays claim to his old territories. It is also said that this wight possesses a crown redolent with immense power; such a prize belongs with a true champion of the gods, not some creaking revenant. You make haste for a monolith deep in the wastes, where sure enough the Wight King and his retinue wait for you. Your quarry offers a brief salute before striding forward, glowing weapon held at the ready. Strike him down and claim your prize.

SET-UP

Prerequisite: 3 dominated territories

Stake: 1 dominated territory

THE WARBANDS
The Challenger and the Adversary player each muster a warband as described in the core rules (Core Book, pg 36), with the following amendments:

1. The Challenger must muster a Chaos warband, and all fighters in the Challenger's warband must be chosen from the Challenger's warband roster.

2. All fighters in the Adversary player's warband must have the **Legions of Nagash** faction runemark (🔮).

3. The leader of the Adversary player's warband must be either a Wight King with Baleful Tomb Blade or Wight King with Black Axe.

3. The combined points value of the fighters in each warband cannot exceed 1,300.

SPECIAL RULES

Ritual Combat: Only the leader of each warband can use abilities or make attack actions that target the leader of the enemy warband.

Draw Upon Ancient Power: At the start of each combat phase, the Adversary player can remove a number of damage points allocated to the leader of their warband equal to the half the number of fighters in their warband (rounding up). For example, if there were 15 fighters in the Adversary player's warband, the Adversary player could remove up to 8 damage points allocated to the leader of their warband.

Bearer of the Crown: The leader of the Adversary player's warband bears the 'Crown of the Barrows' artefact of power (see below).

BATTLEPLAN

Terrain: Draw 3 terrain cards; the Adversary player picks 1 of them to be in play.

Deployment: Frontal Assault

The Challenger's warband uses the blue deployment points.

Victory: Cut off the Head.

Twist: Foreboding Location

THE SPOILS

If the Challenger wins the battle, they can choose 1 of the following spoils:

Treasure Hoard: See page 105.

Artefact of Power: The Challenger can give 1 fighter in their warband the following artefact of power:

Crown of the Barrows: *Amethyst energies swirl around this forbidding crown, seeing those who fall nearby stagger to their feet once more, eyes aglow with witchfire.*

Once per battle, the bearer can use this artefact as an action. If they do so, pick a friendly fighter that has been taken down. Set up that fighter once more on the battlefield wholly within 3" of this fighter. The fighter set up on the battlefield no longer counts as being taken down. Remove 2D6 damage points allocated to that fighter.

THE GROT PURGE

Given the perilous nature of the Eightpoints, it is almost impressive how even here the troglodytic races – grots, troggoths and squigs, to name but a few – have established their clammy kingdoms. These vile creatures are a constant thorn in the side of the Talons of Carngrad; slave caravans are disrupted, treasures looted, and hired war parties disappear without warning.

It is believed that the grots have many lurklairs scattered across the land, their entrances found in ancient ruins surrounded by odorous mould and fluorescent fungus. In the darkness there is no telling where they will emerge from. To further complicate matters, the grots have no doubt set all manner of devious traps to deal with interlopers. Still, should you slay enough of the creatures, it will no doubt blunt their raids for some time – and you can always search their stashes of purloined loot for a reward.

SET-UP

Prerequisite: 3 dominated territories

Stake: 1 dominated territory

THE WARBANDS
The Challenger and the Adversary player each muster a warband as described in the core rules (Core Book, pg 36), with the following amendments:

1. The Challenger must muster a Chaos warband, and all fighters in the Challenger's warband must be chosen from the Challenger's warband roster.

2. All fighters in the Adversary player's warband must have the **Gloomspite Gitz** faction runemark (🦇).

3. The Adversary player's warband can also include any number of thralls with the **Destruction** runemark (🗲).

3. The combined points value of the fighters in each warband cannot exceed 1,300.

SPECIAL RULES

Emerging from the Gloom: At the start of the reserve phase in each battle round, the Adversary player rolls a dice for each fighter from their warband that has been taken down (excluding the leader). On a 5+, an identical fighter is added to the warband and can be set up on the battlefield within 3" of an objective they control.

If the Adversary player's warband controls no objectives, the fighter can instead be set up within 3" of the edge of the battlefield.

BATTLEPLAN

Terrain: Draw 3 terrain cards; the Adversary player picks 1 of them to be in play.

Deployment: Draw a deployment card as normal.

Victory: The Hidden Vault

The Adversary player is the defender.

At the end of the third battle round, the defender reveals which objective marks the hidden vault as normal. However, the battle ends at the end of the fifth battle round. When the battle ends, the player that controls that objective wins the battle.

Twist: Dead of Night

THE SPOILS

If the Challenger wins the battle, they can choose 1 of the following spoils:

Treasure Hoard: See page 105.

Artefact of Power: The Challenger can give 1 fighter in their warband the following artefact of power:

Loonatic Lantern: *A weird glow emanates from this old and rusted lantern, and the longer you hold it the more certain you become that someone is whispering in the back of your mind. Still, despite this, it has an uncanny way of uncovering hidden items of value.*

If the bearer is in your warband, you can re-roll 1 search roll on the lesser artefacts table in the aftermath sequence after each campaign battle.

WARCRY WARBAND ROSTER

WARBAND NAME		GLORY POINTS	DOMINATED TERRITORY

WARBAND ORIGIN	PLAYER NAME

CAMPAIGN QUEST

CAMPAIGN PROGRESS TRACKER

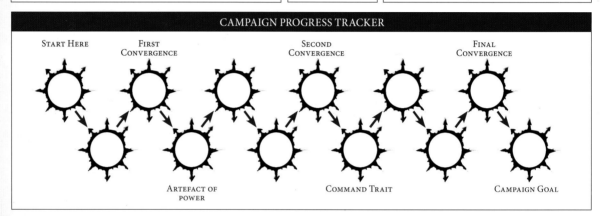

START HERE — FIRST CONVERGENCE — SECOND CONVERGENCE — FINAL CONVERGENCE

ARTEFACT OF POWER — COMMAND TRAIT — CAMPAIGN GOAL

MONSTER

FIGHTER NAME	FIGHTER TYPE	DESTINY LEVELS
		☼ ☼ ☼

HEROES AND ALLIES

FIGHTER NAME	FIGHTER TYPE	ARTEFACTS	DESTINY LEVELS
			☼ ☼ ☼
			☼ ☼ ☼
			☼ ☼ ☼